The Rape of Tutankhamun

The Rape of Tutankhamun

JOHN & ELIZABETH ROMER

LONDON NEW YORK SYDNEY TORONTO

This edition published 1993
by BCA by arrangement with
MICHAEL O'MARA BOOKS

CN 2927

Printed and bound in England
by Clays Limited, St Ives plc

Contents

Acknowledgments

This book has been a long time in the making and extremely difficult to write. Above all we would like to thank Alan Hayling, the splendid Producer/Director of the TV film, *The Rape of Tutankhamun*, for showing us how journalistic investigations are conducted, and above all else for his care and persistence in dealing with a complex and arcane subject. His film is a triumph.

We are especially grateful to those egyptologists who cared sufficiently about conservation to allow themselves to be interviewed by us; Hartwig Altenmüller, François l'Arché, Edwin Brock, Vivian Davies, Peter Dorman, Rosa Frey, Harry James, Christian Leblanc, Arpag Mekhitarian and Don Ryan. We trust that they consider our debate a worthwhile one.

The film, *The Rape of Tutankhamun*, would never have been made were it not for the acute enthusiasm of John Willis of Channel 4 TV, would not have achieved its final form without the care of its editor Sheila MacDowell, its associate producer Noirin ni Dubhgail, and the apt music of Chris Galloway. And it would not have got that far even, without the expert attentions of the camera operator, Brian Sewell, his assistant Pedro 'Badawy' Rodriguez, Rupert Murray, our very sound sound recordist and our two valiant Egyptian facilitators, Romany Helmi and Hamdi Mohammed Moussa. In their own ways, all these people helped us with this book. Thanks are also due, as ever, to Mike O'Mara and his lightning team, the fastest publishers in the west and to the Godfather, Ken Thomson, who made it all possible.

As always, our many friends and colleagues in Egypt aided us at every turn. Above all, we are grateful to them, not only for helping us make a book and film, but for spending their lives caring for a part of all our pasts, and making every trip into that past a truly memorable experience. We remember especially, Dr Mohammed Ibrahim Bakr, Chairman of the Egyptian Antiquities Organization, Dr Zahi Hawass and Dr Elsayed Hegazy: 'Life, Prosperity and Health' to them all.

J. & E. R.

All photographs are the author's, plate 11 being re-photographed from Harry Burton's original print.

Preface & Introduction

1992 was the 70th anniversary of the discovery of Tutankhamun's tomb, a fact that was seized upon and widely celebrated in the media. Professors, journalists, curators and biographers were all united to tell us once again about the magic of the treasure tomb. Very few of these assembled experts though, had anything to say about the present state of that unhappy monument and its Royal Valley, which are both facing disaster.

All in all, there are some eighty-five known tombs in the Valley of the Kings, twenty-five of these being the tombs of the pharaohs of ancient Egypt's elegant New Kingdom period, that is, the period between about 1500–1000 BC. The remaining tombs range from simple pits with rectangular burial chambers to tombs similar to those of the pharaohs, with staircases at their entrances, and corridors, rooms and grand burial chambers at their ending. These were made for senior ministers of state and the intimate friends and family of the king.

Twenty-eight of the presently known tombs in or around the Valley of the Kings were decorated. Many of these survive and some are amongst the finest sculptured and painted monuments of ancient Egypt. Ten of these decorated tombs, however, presently require major conservation. The roots of the problem in this desert valley are twofold: firstly, the valley itself lies on a stratum of shale which is water-sensitive; secondly, the valley is subject to flash floods coming down from the high desert. All but ten of the valley's tombs have been entered by these floods. In the last century and a half, a third of all the known tombs in the valley have been re-buried under rubble and sand brought down by flash floods.

Two-thirds of the tombs, including several of the royal ones, still hold some of this heavy flood debris inside them; and several have been completely filled by it.

It has been more than twenty years since we first wrote upon the Valley of the Kings. Since then, a busy little industry of publication, excavation and conferencing has grown up around it. Nine separate excavators have worked within its forty acres. Fourteen tombs have been opened and cleared or part-cleared of encumbering debris. Presently there are four major excavations underway, ultimately involving the removal of thousands of tons of debris. Others of a similar scale are planned for the near future. Though the rest of the world might regard places like the Royal Valley as wonders, many experts clearly regard them as mines in which to dig for knowledge, as their own words, recorded in this book, will testify. Unfortunately, in the case of the Valley of the Kings, this attitude is now threatening damage to some of the most famous monuments, including the tomb of Tutankhamun itself.

The Valley of the Kings is, of course, a very celebrated place, and it is easy to raise sums of money sufficient to make small excavations in it. After all, there are many known 'lost tombs' there, it has never been completely excavated and the burial places of at least seven pharaohs of the New Kingdom period have yet to be discovered. To potential sponsors then, excavating the Royal Valley may offer exciting possibilities of new discoveries; to its excavators, the good chance that, as most things in the Royal Valley were connected with the person of pharaoh, even the smallest find may be of significance. Even on this level however, to the concern of many in the egyptological community, the professional standards of some of these archaeologists are low; one experienced commentator has described some of the recent excavations as 'dubious undertakings, destroying more than they recover'.

This, then, is the Rape of Tutankhamun: the exploitation of a small valley in a foreign country by a diverse group of specialists who, in return, give precious little to conserve its ancient monuments, and worse, on occasion, even seem to threaten them. Tutankhamun, then, is raped by science or, at least, an outdated science, similar in many ways to zoology in the days of the great white hunters.

The Egyptian Antiquities Organization (EAO), the hard-pressed governmental agency with responsibility for the care of all the Egyptian monuments, has specifically appealed for foreign help in the work of conservation. So far, the response has been minimal.

If ancient Egypt is really to be conserved, and conserved in its own landscapes; if its hundred pyramids, five hundred temples, and ten thousand tombs are to survive – and many of these are stressed and threatened now as they have never been before – it will require more effort and know-how than any single country could possibly muster. Both the expertise and the will to help exists already in the west, but it simply is not mobilized. Public pressure, alerted by the media, needs to ensure it will be. And this must happen soon, if the ancient world and its relics are to survive the modern world.

The term Valley of the Kings used below refers only to the Eastern Valley of the Wadi Bibân el-Mulûk, that is, the part that tourists come to see. Though suffering the assaults of both archaeologists and movie companies, the Western Valley and its tombs are not threatened in the same ways as their more famous counterparts.

The 'I' of the text refers to both its authors: after close encounters with the dull essays of committees, we have rendered ourselves singular. We hope that our text, based upon long observation and investigations in the majestic Valley of the Kings, experiences that have now moved us to write this book, also speaks with a single voice. We hope too, that this voice is clear enough to promote a much-needed debate but, above all, that it may serve in some small way to help our friends in Egypt to save their heritage.

This, then, is the history of the menacing and mutilation of one of the most beautiful places on earth, the Valley of the Kings at Thebes, in Upper Egypt.

John and Elizabeth Romer
Aiola, Tuscany, 30 July 1993

CHAPTER I

A Brief Tour of the Treasure

IN THE BEGINNING

From a dry, dusty, Upper Egyptian valley in the year 1922, the news of the discovery of the Tomb of Tutankhamun flashed around the world and excited the imaginations of all who heard it.

In the brilliant light, against the limestone wall, the colors of all these things were vibrant yet soft – a medley of brown, yellow, blue, amber, gold, russet and black.

Such were the memories of a young American boy who had the extraordinary good fortune to be shown the first chamber of the tomb of Tutankhamun just days after its initial opening. Howard Carter, its somewhat phlegmatic excavator, had instructed his visitors, fellow archaeologists, to be at the Valley at three in the afternoon, arriving there by a circuitous route to avoid unwanted attention, and bringing with them a complete change of underclothes as the temperature in the tomb was so high that even a brief stay there caused copious perspiration. 'To relieve the curious tension of the moment', the small group made commonplace, nervous conversation before following Carter down the short descent into the interior. The boy, the young son of James Henry Breasted, perhaps the greatest of all American egyptologists, remembered how Carter sounded as he spoke to them, his recollection still genuine and fresh before a lifetime's re-tellings of the tale:

His imagination recaptured the emotion of that first moment, and his voice failed him. He paused for a moment...We understood – for as he sat describing in a low voice what he had seen in those first moments, we too found ourselves deeply stirred.

Once in the tomb, so moved were the group by their first sight of the undreamt-of treasure that tears came to their eyes.

Imagine how it must have been a few days earlier, on 26 November 1922, when Carter had walked down those sixteen cream-white steps of the tomb to open the sealed doorway for the first time. Eminent professors who had passed their entire lives ruminating on the wealth and power of ancient pharaohs were completely unprepared for the vision that Carter revealed. Breasted, more imaginative, more urbane, than most of his colleagues, was completely dazzled. Years later, his son recorded the precise moment when Carter showed his father's party that first roomful of treasure:

All my life I shall remember the picture of that little group of men as they stood waiting with glowing eyes while Carter paused...and suddenly drew the white sheet away.

At that moment, it must have seemed to them as if something of the very heart of the Egyptian mystery had been revealed:

...we saw an incredible vision, an impossible scene from a fairy tale, an enchanted property-room from the opera house of some great composer's dreams. Opposite us were three couches upon which a king had lain, all about were chests, caskets, alabaster vases, gold-embellished stools and chairs – the heaped-up riches of a Pharaoh who had died some three thousand, two hundred years ago...when Carter said...'will you not enter?' they were reluctant to move lest everything vanish like a mirage. Still hesitant, they went in very slowly and...stood for some time as if transfixed, their incredulous gaze taking in the entire room. When at last they turned and looked into Carter's face, to whom it was no longer new, the experience was overpoweringly moving.

Of that extraordinary day, Breasted himself could only remember that, as he stood amidst the gold, he uttered one exclamation after another, and then turned again to shake Carter's hand...Here was the magnificence, which only the wealth and splendor of the Imperial Age in Egypt in the fourteenth century before Christ could have wrought or conceived – and as it at first seemed, with everything still standing as if it was placed there when the tomb was last closed.

As a professional egyptologist, Breasted was also anxious to record the vision:

Emotion struggled with the habit of years to observe and to understand, a struggle in which my critical faculties were for the moment completely routed. All about us lay a totally new revelation of ancient life.

Aimlessly, the great man fingered his notebook and pencil:

Of what use were notes made in such a state of mind, what myriad details and whirling thoughts crowding to be recorded all at once. There, between two of the couches stood four alabaster vases...No-one had ever seen such vases before. Yonder was a casket of jewelry, and under one of the couches lay a courtier's magnificent baton with a superb handle of gleaming gold... The splendour of Nineveh and Babylon seems now but a rough foil for setting off the civilization of Egyptian Thebes, which could boast such craftsmen as had produced this royal furniture – men quite worthy to stand beside Lorenzo Ghiberti and Benvenuto Cellini. I felt the traditional 'culture values' of the ancient world shifting so rapidly that it made me fairly dizzy.

Today it is possible to visit the Cairo Museum and feel something of the same jolt of wonder that so amazed the first visitors to the tomb when we too gaze at Tutankhamun's accoutrements as they lie sparkling in the daylight.

King Solomon's Mines, The Mummy and a thousand other nineteenth-century romances might have prepared the west for such a vision. But in the event, they had not. This new-found ancient Egypt simply beggared all earlier visions of the past. Appearing miraculously and completely unannounced in an Upper Egyptian valley, ancient Egypt had re-invented itself. In four stuffy rooms still filled with the same draughts of desert air that the ancient mourners had breathed at the time of funeral, lay all the preserved paraphernalia of pharaoh, exposed now, for modern delectation.

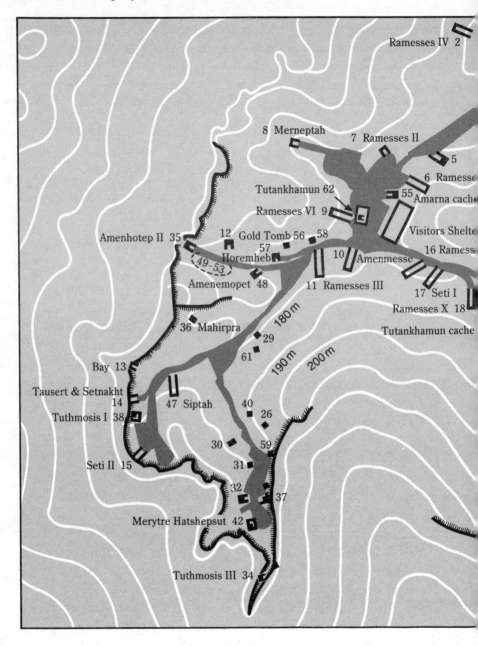

Ramesses IV 2

8 Merneptah
7 Ramesses II
5
6 Ramesse

Tutankhamun 62
55 Amarna cache
Ramesses VI 9
Visitors Shelte

Amenhotep II 35
12
Gold Tomb 56   58
57
Horemheb
49-53
Amenemopet 48
10 Amenmesse
16 Ramess
11 Ramesses III
17 Seti I
Ramesses X 18

36 Mahirpra
180 m
29
Tutankhamun cache
61
190 m
200 m

Bay 13

Tausert & Setnakht
14
47 Siptah
40
26
Tuthmosis I 38

30
59
Seti II 15
31

32
37

Merytre Hatshepsut 42

Tuthmosis III 34

Heaps of chariots, statues, thrones, glittering shrines all filled with gods and, of course, jewels beyond belief. Perhaps yet more wonderful even than this, beside these golden trappings of statehood, lay the very corpse of the King himself, his two stillborn children, and all the fragile ephemera of ancient life. The toys and clothing and the underclothing that Tutankhamun himself had worn in life; his chairs and bedding too, and all the furniture of daily life. All those elegant and playful things, in fact, that for the last thirty years have decorated Tutankhamun shows from Moscow to New York; in Tokyo, Berlin, Paris and London; in Toronto, Hanover, Leningrad and Richmond; in Virginia, Hamburg, Houston and all the rest.

As a Disney executive recently observed to me, 'Nowadays, ancient Egypt is big business'. In truth, Tutankhamun's reappearance in western Thebes not only served to re-invent ancient Egypt in the imagination of the west, but also spawned new ways of approaching and marketing the past. For the Tutankhamun shows of the 1970s initiated a brand new genre of exhibition: the 'blockbuster', named perhaps as much after the patient people who wait in lines long enough to wind around the blocks in which the great museums stand as for the bombs of the Second World War. This new Tutankhamun, blockbuster Tutankhamun, you could call him, was the brainchild of a British book packager, George Rainbird, who sensed that, in the first age of cheap colour printing and colour TV, Tutankhamun's dusty gold lying in Cairo Museum might be as much to the taste of the western public of the 1970s as it had been to their grandparents some fifty years before.

Curiously enough, by the 1950s it was very far from the tastes of many professionals. Most egyptologists and many art historians, too, considered Tutankhamun's treasures to be overblown and rather vulgar. There were also distant memories of the scandals and lawsuits that had accompanied the tomb's opening, to say nothing of the unsavoury rumours of treasures taken from the tomb and sold illicitly to several museums in the west where they now resided in full public view, though labelled with suitably scholarly ambiguity to hide their precise date and provenance.

More than this even, royal tombs were simply out of fashion. Most egyptologists, indeed, regarded the Valley of the Kings and its tombs as a somewhat tedious relic, of little historical interest – I still remember the surprise that my continued visits to the Royal Valley occasioned amongst the older egyptologists on the expedition on which I worked in the 1960s. Furthermore, at that same time, Tutankhamun's homeland was about as fashionable for tourists as Iraq and Libya are today. Allied to the USSR, Nasser and revolutionary post-Suez Egypt were not held in great esteem by the western media. None the less, George Rainbird persevered. First he had a fine set of colour photographs prepared, the first ever made of the treasures, and he commissioned a special book for them. At the same time, he floated the notion at the British Museum and at *The Times* newspaper (which, in Carter's day, had enjoyed exclusive rights at the tomb) that an international exhibition of the Egyptian treasures would be a sensation.

Rainbird was right, of course. The book, *Tutankhamun, Life and Death of a Pharaoh*, became a bestseller and the idea of international Tutankhamun shows caught on like wildfire. Like Picasso's paintings and the New England fall, the golden mask looked very good in Kodachrome and on TV, and it soon became the icon of the international exhibition and even, by association, of ancient Egypt itself. Soon unseemly struggles broke out amongst western museum curators, each one attempting to exhibit the treasures before the other. Would the golden coffin go to Brooklyn? The mask to Hildesheim? The throne to Tokyo? Eminent museum conservators were enlisted to report that the ancient woods that underlaid the treasures' golden foil were strong enough to travel to the world's museums, or if they were not, that the ancient things were so imperiled by decay that a journey to the laboratories of these same museums was essential for their conservation (and then perhaps, though who could guess, for exhibition too!). Ambassadors around the world were wined and dined. Heads of state were co-opted onto mythical committees designed to steer the golden treasures on their way.

The ultimate Tutankhamun shows, with the glossiest catalogues and a deluge of glittery souvenirs, were the US exhibitions of 1976–9. By this time, ten years' experience of blockbusting had shown the organizers that exclusive images of the objects, that is, the movie rights and high quality colour photographs, were worth far more to them than the ancient treasures would have been. Today, retired Egyptian officials of the Egyptian Antiquities Organization remember the arrogance of those exhibition organizers, once armed with the letters of release that had been issued over the formers' heads. And their successors ruefully repeat the commonly held belief that, of the funds generated by those exhibitions and their marketing – almost $120 million, it is said – only $9 million ever found its way home to Egypt. Whether such figures are accurate or not, one thing is surely true: just as he had been in the years after his discovery, Tutankhamun had once again become a vital element of the world's cultural landscape. At a recent count, some eighty films have been made about the young king, and 400-odd books published on his tomb and its treasures.

Tutankhamun's gold has rubbed off, too, on all the rest of ancient Egypt, a sustaining gleam that has inadvertently aided the perennially strapped profession of egyptology. Just as there must be very few egyptologists today who were not attracted to their subject through childhood glimpses of the treasures of the boy king, so, for egyptology itself, Tutankhamun serves as a handle upon the popular imagination. And as donations to professional bodies have grown and grown, other would-be blockbuster pharaohs come fast upon us. So Ramesses II has become 'the Great' and Amenhotep III, 'the Magnificent', and the arts of their two reigns have attracted mass audiences. 'In 1987,' my Disney executive told me, 'more people saw the Ramesses the Great show in Dallas, Texas than went to see the Dallas Cowboys during the same period of time.'

These shimmering images of treasures, the all-night queues, the films and books and all the clever exhibitions, have also served to put Egypt back at the centre of the map of world tourism; at the centre, that is, of the world's largest and fastest growing industry. In the late 1970s, loans from the World Bank aided the building of hotels and airports to cater for the ever-growing throngs of visitors. Hundreds of cruise boats were built to carry passengers up and down the Nile to visit the wondrous temples that lie like basking lizards right through the desert valley. Nowadays, more than two million tourists visit the standing monuments of Egypt every year. A novel highlight of a trip to modern Luxor is a 'balloon experience', an hour's voyage at dawn that provides a splendid view of the sun rising over the ancient city and the Valley of the Kings. Appropriately enough, the balloon bears as decoration a massive golden painting of Tutankhamun's golden mask.

With this sort of stardom, with this level of international interest and involvement, you might imagine that, like Madonna and the Dallas Cowboys, like rainforests and whales, ancient Egypt would be carefully observed by its professionals, and even pampered, too. This, however, has not been the case: Tutankhamun and his tomb and treasures have suffered badly. Forty-six major blockbusters have left some of the tomb's treasures severely damaged. Before the Egyptian Government wisely put a stop to their international exhibition, conservators travelling with Tutankhamun's treasures had sometimes to reconstruct the disintegrating objects as they were taken from their cases at each new venue. And in the Valley of the Kings at Luxor, a world-class tourist attraction now, more damage has been done to the royal tombs since Howard Carter's day than in all the previous millennia of their existence.

In all of this, the single most disconcerting thing is that those whom you might presume to be the guardians of our past, its curators and professors, are not much interested in this slow destruction. They prefer to conduct long and learned correspondences upon such topics as the minutiæ of regal successions, or the identities of the original owners of Valley tombs or, in a more social vein, a Keeper at the British Museum may proudly announce the restoration of Howard Carter's own tomb in Putney Cemetery. Enterprises like the international conference held in June 1990 at Lord Carnarvon's stately home, Highclere, to celebrate the 75th anniversary of the beginning of the search for the golden tomb are well attended, but not one professional from the west has cared enough about the physical reality of the monuments themselves even to remark in public that, as they spoke, the Royal Valley and its tombs were facing the severest threat to their existence they had ever known. Less than a year after the High-clere conference, on New Year's Day 1991, Tutankhamun's tomb was lightly flooded for the first time in its entire existence, a sad, significant event that was passed over completely in the dozens of scholarly journals and magazines of egyptology – the same journals that report the progress of the five modern expeditions then working in the Royal Valley, close to Tutankhamun's tomb.

Clearly, in itself, scholarship is an interesting and blameless activity but should it not be allied to an active concern for the monuments themselves? In their ivory towers most scholars and archaeologists hardly seem to notice the continuing physical decay of the sites that they have chosen to study. With few honourable exceptions western academe has not rushed to help its Egyptian colleagues in their increasingly unequal struggle to preserve the monuments of Egypt.

Recently, the Getty Conservation Institute, which specializes in archaeological conservation worldwide, has devised a scheme to save the fast deteriorating walls of Tutankhamun's tomb, its plaster loosened now, its paint a little smudged and washed away. Yet no amount of skilled cosmetic work can alter the fact that the rock in which Tutankhamun's tomb and all the other tombs of the Royal Valley are situated is now in movement and, in consequence of this, many of the tombs are cracking and starting, very slowly, to collapse.

TUTANKHAMUN FLOODED, SETI EXCAVATED

After numerous ancient funeral parties had arranged and rearranged, and checked and sealed and shut, and then finally re-sealed the little tomb of Tutankhamun, nothing would enter it for three thousand years and more. Neither mouse nor moth, nor air nor water; the hard plaster on the doorways of the tomb served as a hermetic seal. In a publication of 1926, one of Carter's assistants, the chemist Arthur Lucas, carefully noted that

...the morning after the sealed door of the burial chamber was opened, sterile swabs were taken...of these five...four were sterile and the fifth contained

a few organisms that were undoubtably air-infections unavoidably introduced during the opening...it may be accepted that no bacterial life whatever
was present...Not only was bacterial life absent, but life in any form.

After the tomb's final closing, then, the oxygen inside had slowly
diminished. Insects that had entered with the burial parties, even
the yeasts and bacteria in the tomb, had all died.

In chemical and physical reactions spanning thousands of
years, largely resulting from the desiccation of the small quantities of water from the plants and woods and textiles in the tomb,
from the breath of the ancient burial parties, from the corn that
had germinated in the tomb, and from the wines and food that
had been piled there, all the tomb's contents had changed but
most had suffered no great violence. In the first room a mysterious pink colour had been blasted over the floors and walls alike.
Similarly, the plastered walls of the burial chamber were dotted
with dark spots which, though inert at the time of its opening,
had the appearance of having grown like lichen in the dark.
Despite such eerie crucibles, for the most part the objects in the
tomb had stayed intact. As for the tomb itself, its floors and walls
and ceilings all cut out of living rock, this, along with the very
landscape of the valley itself, had also been caught up in similarly
slow processes of change and movement. In such millennial
alchemies though, such things as do occur are very subtle and
often imperceptible. Certainly, none of them are due simply to the
passing 'hand of time'.

Every change has its cause. In places like the Valley of the Kings,
most violent damage has come to the tombs abruptly and with
physical disasters such as floods and earthquakes or, more
recently, with mass tourism, with plundering and uncaring
archaeology. Specifically, most of the damage that the Valley of the
Kings has suffered, and yet still suffers, comes from the first and
last of this list of afflictions.

Running diagonally across the limestone ceiling of Tutankhamun's burial chamber is an ancient rock fault which, in earlier geological ages, once carried water down along it. As the
ancient masons quarried out the tomb, they had to contend with

crystals lying in this fault, hard crystals formed by the passage of these ancient waters. You may clearly see the results of the quarrymen's struggle with this hard vein in the soft limestone, which must have bent and sometimes even fractured their soft copper chisels. At all events, the vein was never properly levelled off with the rest of the ceiling. So, as you stand on the modern viewing platform looking down towards the golden coffin, you may see it still hanging there, just above your head. As the quarrymen hammered at these crystals though, they loosened some of the nearby limestone, which then fell away; the finger marks the masons left on the coarse plaster that they threw into these holes in a attempt to roughly level the ceiling, are still quite clear and sharp. This plaster also served to seal up the ancient rock fault. For three thousand years and more, this seal remained unbroken, even finally witnessing Carter's dismantling of the great golden shrines and splendid spangled canopies that, for all the time the burial was undisturbed, lay just a few feet beneath, and perfectly dry.

In 1991, however, water from a severe rainstorm penetrated this ancient rock fault, ran along the line of crystals in the tomb, then down the walls. And as it ran, it stained and washed away some of the pigment of the painted figure of Tutankhamun's *ka*, a part of the spirit of the boy king. When the storm was over, some three inches of water lay on the floor of the burial chamber all around the king's sarcophagus, water that was finally bailed out by local EAO officials and a conservation student who happened to be present on that day. Sixty years earlier, Arthur Lucas had observed that, up until that time, there had been no evidence of water penetration 'into the tomb at any time'. While it is probably true that since the 1920s some stray rain water has indeed trickled down under the door and along the open corridors of the tomb – I myself saw some running down the entrance stairs in 1979 and there was no reason to think that this was a unique event – the 1991 flood that came in through the tomb's roof seems to have been the first occurrence of its kind. And that is sad, because a further rainstorm and flooding will surely serve to loosen and to stain further larger sections of the tomb's rear wall which clearly cannot support such heavy soakings.

Yet the damage that water may do in places like Tutan-khamun's burial chamber extends way beyond washing the paint-ings and their plaster from the walls. Over the millennia, water has triggered the destruction of many of the largest tombs in the Val-ley. In sufficient quantity, it causes the very rocks of the valley to heave and twist and split. Most of the violent destruction that has visited the royal tombs in the last three thousand years has been caused by freak flash floods crashing through the tomb doors or filling the tombs like that of Tutankhamun with water deriving from distant desert rainfalls and filtering down long rock faults which serve as natural desert drains. All this has long been known by those who cared to look. The ancient quarrymen, for example, learnt from hard experience to make provision for such catast-rophes. But such experience cannot explain this particular event: why was it that on New Year's Day 1991 a single long-closed fault in Tutankhamun's tomb, one sealed at least since the time of the royal burial, should suddenly heave and crack its ancient plaster sealing and start to leak fresh water? The answer is indicated by a general pattern of novel damage that has been occurring in the Valley of the Kings over the past twenty years or so.

For it is not just Tutankhamun's tomb that has suffered recent cracking and flooding. There are twenty-four more royal tombs running off the desert paths of the Valley – and many of them, too, have recently been moving and cracking and leaking. In one tomb at least, one of the finest tombs in Egypt, water has also brought down part of a unique burial chamber ceiling, celebrated since the days when it was found. This pattern of recent, rapid and quite new damage running right across the Valley points to specific recent causes – that is, to recent physical changes in the Valley of the Kings. Now, for the past thirty years or so, these have been limited in the Valley to a small number of factors. One direct cause, however, known in at least two cases to have provoked serious cracking and collapses, is archaeological excavation. When it is recognized that at the present time –1993 – there are several expe-ditions working close to Tutankhamun's tomb with no equipment to monitor change or movements in the tombs at all, you may rightly feel some cause for concern.

To see the devastating effects of earlier uncontrolled excavations in the Valley, you have only to walk out of Tutankhamun's tomb, out into the bright, white desert light, and up a chalky path for forty yards or so and down the staircases of the great tomb of Seti I. Since 1960, the world-famous decorations in this tomb have been cracking and falling with a sinister regularity and with no foreseeable sign of stopping. Most of this damage is directly attributable to recent archaeology conducted in the tomb; in 1960, an excavation partly cleared a mysterious corridor which had been filled from floor to roof with rock-hard debris brought down in ancient floods. The beginning of the mysterious corridor was itself already more than 90 metres from the doorway of the tomb, and more than 25 metres lower in the ground. Before the excavators stopped, beaten by a lack of oxygen and the fatigues and miseries and lack of funds that frequently attend such labours, they had penetrated another 136 metres into the Valley cliff and descended 75 metres further into the ground. The opening up of this corridor served to dry and desiccate the rock in which King Seti's tomb is cut. And this today, some thirty years on, is still causing parts of the tomb to twist and split and fall.

In truth, this work of excavation, which consisted of the driving of a rough tunnel through the hard-packed flood debris that had choked the precise architecture of the ancient tunnel, was badly done. Nor did the excavator supervise his workmen properly: years

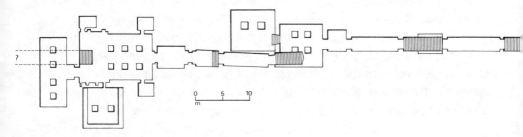

A sketch plan of the tomb of Seti I. The mouth of the corridor excavated by Sheik Ali Abd er Rassul, shown in dotted line, runs down from the floor of the burial chamber (*see* Plate 10), and under the White Room, which has collapsed (*see* Plate 11)

later, you could still find small fragments of royal funerary equipment, like shattered little pieces of Tutankhamun's treasures, offered unknowingly for sale in local antiquities shops. Doubtless, larger and finer pieces from the dig had circulated earlier in the auction rooms of London and Zurich. Neither was the work scientifically recorded, being overseen and financed not by an academic, but by a local hotel proprietor, Sheik Ali Abd er Rassul, a descendent of the three famous brothers who, in the 1870s, had discovered and plundered a cache of kings that had been taken from their tombs in the Valley of the Kings and hidden in the Theban cliffs. For ten years and more, these three brothers had sold their royal treasures through a British consular agent in Luxor to the European museums; a fact that eighty years on, had led Sheik Ali to the belief that he shared some deep affinity and common purpose with those august institutions. Just a moderate number of Egyptian pounds, the Sheik would say, would buy you a glimpse of the family's last remaining royal treasure: a queen's papyrus from his family's great discovery, held back by his ancestors from the examining magistrates who tortured and tormented the secret of the tomb's location from them. The subsequent story of these royal mummies is well enough recorded: badly excavated by European egyptologists, the ancient pharaohs, the Ramesses, the Amenhoteps and many other Theban kings, were taken off to Cairo for exhibition in the new museum, and to be studied and published in monograph and photograph and X-rays too, by foreign egyptologists.

For a while though, in the late 1960s, for just a very brief period in post-revolutionary Egypt, the tables were turned on this alien academy and the heirs of the tomb's discoverers were once again given their head amongst the golden hills of Thebes. Unfortunately however, the vision proved to be a mirage. Such secrets as the brothers had hidden from their inquisitors were long since lost and, like Alexander with his army, Sheik Ali was finally forced to abandon his eternal excavation when his work-force simply refused to continue working in the long dark dangerous tunnel they had carved out of the tomb. And so he left the Valley disappointed but always vowing to return, and this desire was often expressed in lengthy telegrams addressed to the President of Egypt. The old Sheik died a few years ago, the last, perhaps, of a remarkable line and sorely missed not only by his family but also by his foreign friends, to whom he seemed to be almost as old and as intractable as the hills around his house.

In the winter of 1959–60 though, even as the Sheik's men still fought their way through the rock-hard debris of the corridor, the humidity levels in the rock underlying the decorated sections in which King Seti's tomb was cut began to change. Quite quickly, the freshly exposed rocks began to desiccate and shrink and fall. Long, thin, horizontal cracks began to open in the burial chamber walls. Then, in the height of summer, just a few years after the Sheik's departure from the tomb, a large white-walled room that lay behind the royal burial chamber and over Sheik Ali's long dark corridor suddenly collapsed. This spare and elegant room had, but for the carcass of a great bull slaughtered at King Seti's funeral and a mass of names that innumerable European travellers had scratched and pencilled on its perfect walls, been completely empty. Now, great horizontal cracks opened right along its walls, the four huge square columns that stood in single line right down its centre dropped away from the ceiling of the room and, in consequence of this, great slabs of stone fell down from the roof. Part of the floor directly over the lower corridor gave way completely. In a few days, a perfect ancient interior had taken on the appearance of a natural cavern. Scarcely had the local antiquities officers had time to fill the room with wooden supporting beams – beams which still hold up this sad interior today – when portions of nearby rooms in the tomb, some of them covered in exquisite low relief, started to collapse as well. Collapse, just as they had done fifty years before Sheik Ali's work when another excavator, the young Howard Carter, had started the clearance of that same fatal lower corridor. He, however, realized his mistake and stopped when the chamber started to split and move.

Thirty years and more after Sheik Ali's excavation, the royal burial chamber and the rooms around it are still moving. In 1991, following the same heavy rainfall that damaged Tutankhamun's tomb, large slabs of the burial chamber's beautiful astronomical ceiling fell onto the floor and smashed to smithereens. Sections of the starred ceilings from other rooms, too, had fallen previously and disintegrated; parts of a stone cornice in another room as well, and a doorway too, have simply fallen down. And there is no reason at all now, to think that this melancholy process has miraculously stopped. Stress gauges show that part of the rooms which previously have not suffered much are now in greater movement than the rest, while fresh water stains upon the sound end of the burial chamber vault show that fresh collapses should be expected there, perhaps after the next rains have penetrated the faulted rocks of the chamber roof and soaked the loosened blocks, making them heavier than usual, and thus more liable to fall.

Within a week of the devastating collapse of 1991, the Chairman of the Egyptian Antiquities Organization, Dr Mohammed Ibrahim Bakr, gave an opening address to the Sixth International Congress of Egyptology at Turin, Italy, in which he invited foreign archaeologists to help in the urgent work of conservation of Egypt's monuments. He singled out for special mention the vulnerability of tombs in the Valley of the Kings.

Privately, in the conference corridors, Egyptian officials were also voicing further concerns. Yet not one of the western delegates so much as mentioned the collapse, indeed Dr Bakr seemed to earn himself a mild rebuke from the chair of the conference, who told him in reply that the primary purpose of the gathering was egyptology not conservation. And that, unhappily, was true enough: of the 340 papers delivered at that conference, just three of them were on site conservation.

Though the decision to grant Sheik Ali a licence to excavate among the royal tombs had been ruled more by the heart than by the head, if truth be told, in the present state of academia, if Sheik Ali had graduated with honours in egyptology from Oxford or from Yale, the end results of his labours would have been much the same. Scientifically observed, the meagre treasures extracted from that gloomy tunnel seem merely to have been washed down into it by ancient floods and could tell us precious little about the great king or his wondrous tomb. As for the damage that the excavation is still causing to the famous chambers in the tomb above; in all the world, there is not a degree course in egyptology that would have served to warn him of the perils of such work. Not one of them requires a qualification in site conservation, let alone the elementary knowledge of rock mechanics which could have served to indicate the dire results of such an enterprise. To amplify these extraordinary facts, and show their relevance within the royal tombs today: at the present time – in 1993 – there are several foreign excavations whose work in broadly similar geological locations in the Royal Valley is well underway, and several more are planned to start quite soon. To be sure, these modern excavations have not been undertaken in the same spirit as Sheik Ali's venture. These are serious scientific enterprises, overseen by western archaeologists, working soberly and seriously in the name of science. Yet their work has precisely the same potential for devastating the Valley and its tombs as did that of the Sheik and his men. Already, tell-tale cracks have started to appear in many of the tombs.

'Presently there are five missions working in the Valley of the Kings,' says Dr Elsayed Hegazy, the Director General of Antiquities at Qurna, western Thebes, 'but not one of them is co-operating with us to save the monuments. Everyone wants to publish a tomb, but no-one wants to study its geology. They don't want to restore it, or pay for glass to protect it from visitors. Up until now, the Egyptian Antiquities Organization has worked in the Valley of the Kings alone.'

'CLOSED FOR RESTORATION'

The more or less continuous pattern of damage in the Valley of the Kings has meant that, for years now, many of the royal tombs have been intermittently 'closed for restoration', a familiar enough message these days, right throughout the world. In Egypt too, it is far more than the Theban royal tombs that are 'closed for restoration'.

The struggle to 'Save the Sphinx' has, of course, been international news for years. The rest of the problem, however, is not so well known. Just like the Sphinx though, the majority of Egypt's temples have only been freed from their protecting sand and the accretions of ages within the past two centuries. Exposed for the first time in thousands of years, wind and temperature changes and, increasingly, various forms of chemical pollution have been stealthily eroding their surfaces ever since – a slow attrition that is now beginning to cause major losses to their wall surfaces.

Inevitably, modern development is also threatening the ancient monuments. At the time the Pyramids were built, just one or two million people lived beside the Nile in Egypt: now the figure is close to 60 million. The burgeoning village in the shadow of the Pyramids of Giza received piped water a few years ago. This led to a rise of the subterranean water table which, laden with salts and other chemicals, spread out under the Sphinx. For a while, this was a major factor in its recent deterioration. Changing irrigation patterns also serve to keep the foundations of many of the ancient monuments permanently soaked in water and this, too, for the first time in their long existence. This water not only weakens stone and hence the ancient walls and columns, but also enables corrosive salts to break through its surface, as happened at the Sphinx. Thus, though the 1992 earthquake damaged more Islamic monuments than pharaonic ones, the harm that was done to them allowed a melancholy glimpse of the future. Here and there, odd blocks of previously weakened stone fell from pyramids and temples: fragile ancient town sites were severely damaged. The ultimate effect of the earthquake on the tombs, however, is still largely unknown.

One thing though is true of all this sad catalogue: with few exceptions, when it comes to the repair and replacement of fallen walls and columns, for the most part the Egyptians have to manage quite alone. It is fortunate for the world heritage that they are both skilful and resourceful.

The scale of the task facing the Egyptian Antiquities Organization (EAO) is extraordinary. Egypt's pharaonic antiquities are dealt with by just one of various departments which between them govern the country's kaleidoscope of cultures – ancient Egyptian, Græco–Roman, Coptic, and Islamic. By itself, the load of the pharaonic section would be impressive. The official in charge of the Valley of the Kings, for example, Dr Elsayed Hegazy, not only bears responsibility for the royal tombs, but also for some forty temples and more than four hundred private tombs, as well as all the other numerous ancient monuments on the west Bank of the Nile opposite modern Luxor. Similarly large numbers of monuments stand on the east bank too; other sites, some with equal concentrations of antiquity, run down both sides of the Nile and through the Delta to the Mediterranean Sea. At a rough estimate – and it is very rough indeed – Egypt has a hundred major pyramids, five hundred large stone temples and thousands of fragile, decorated, ancient tombs; then there are the Græco-Roman monuments, Coptic monasteries and the fabulous wealth of Islamic Cairo. As well as this, of course, there are the museums, which lie thick and fast upon the land, some of them containing the most celebrated collections of their kind in the world. Though some 15,000 government employees care for this enormous patrimony, the truth is that there are probably more ancient monuments in Egypt than there are employees to care for them.

Tourism of course, ever enlarging, does its share of damage and its management takes up large amounts of the department's resources and time. Presently, the number of visitors to Egypt every year is roughly equal to the entire ancient population of the country when it was engaged upon building pyramids. In the 1960s, Luxor airport was little more than an airstrip. Now jumbo-loads of visitors fly right to the heart of ancient Thebes, and the huge Boeings bank high over the Valley of the Kings.

Each year, the EAO expends colossal sums on maintenance and conservation – a heroic effort by a burgeoning, emerging nation beset with a host of modern problems. Most of these funds derive from the sale of tickets to sites and to museums, which is very good business in those years when Egypt is perceived to be a safe holidaying ground by foreign travellers. Despite the fact that numerous foreign missions presently work among the standing monuments of pharaonic Egypt, staffed by professionals who gain their living from studying the ancient culture, the foreign contribution to the upkeep of ancient Egypt is minimal. Egyptian Government regulations require some conservation efforts of them, and so they may all claim to be conservators of ancient Egypt. Despite a few honourable exceptions, however – these primarily funded directly from their governments – most attitudes to conservation amongst the foreign visitors range from the alarmed 'But, conservation is too expensive,' (conversation, Swiss archaeologist, Valley of the Kings) to the canny use of popular conservation terminology for raising funds to continue that most traditional of egyptological pastimes, the production of large volumes of line drawings of ancient paintings and relief. 'Time has never seemed so pressing in our struggle to save the monuments of pharaonic Egypt,' (pamphlet, University of Chicago). Here we have inadvertently entered the topsy-turvy world of egyptological jargon, where conservation is not always what you might think. Many egyptologists, for example, believe that 'conservation' can be the act of describing something in a book; as the Keeper of Egyptian Antiquities at the British Museum, Dr Vivian Davis – joint editor of a well-received publication, *Problems and Priorities in Egyptian Archaeology* – recently observed, 'There is more than one way of conserving a site, in my view the best way is to document it properly, record it and publish it'.

Such attitudes are widely held and taught in western museums and universities, so it is hardly surprising that the excavation of ancient Egypt continues apace while many excavated monuments stand in distress. Indeed, today there are more funds available than ever before, and there are more expeditions working too, digging more and more of ancient Egypt from the protecting earth. It is hardly surprising then that, like so many of the tombs in the Valley of the Kings, increasing amounts of ancient Egypt are now 'closed for restoration'. As Dr Zahi Hawass, an official of the EAO recently observed, unless the present efforts in conservation are greatly increased, 'in a century the paintings will be gone, and in two centuries, the architecture will be gone, too'. Here then, is where the real problems and priorities of modern Egyptian archaeology are to be found.

WHY CARE?

Why in the world should we westerners be especially bothered with such ancient things in distant countries? Is there anything more for most people than an æsthetic thrill that can be bought much more easily for the price of a museum ticket? The truth, of course, is that there is: places like the ruin fields of Egypt are as an important a part of this planet as are its birds and animals. Such relics stand at our beginnings and, by showing us something of our beginnings, they can help us better understand ourselves.

'Do you not know,' says an Egyptian scribe as ancient Egypt was coming to its ending, 'that Egypt is a copy of heaven and the temple of the whole world?' He knew, as did many writers of his day, that some of the forms and institutions invented in his ancient landscape had become the foundations on which the brand-new states in Greece and all along the eastern Mediterranean had built their individual characters and dignity: forms and institutions that today seem so basic to us that many people think of them as 'human nature'.

As for the royal tombs of Thebes, some of the most subtle aspects of our history are held in them, amongst the starry ceilings and on their carved and sculpted walls. Taken as a whole, the Valley tombs can help us to understand the roots of our wide and deeply held belief that human life has form and meaning. They may also help us to understand the order of that form and meaning in which the west has such belief: something of the beginnings of the modern mind is held within the very spaces of the golden valley, in the halls and corridors of its shadowed tombs.

Death engenders the most serious and sombre of human activities: at times of burial people act in earnest. And usually, what they express in thoughts and actions is something of their most elemental beliefs. Sometimes, these beliefs may be but half understood – why, for example, leave flowers at a mother's grave – but none the less they are often felt to be essential. In the Valley of the Kings you may observe the ancient Egyptian state, the world's first, in extremis. Observe it at that most delicate of times, when the very personification of their state, the pharaoh, had died.

Observe the setting in motion of those events, the actions and the rituals, the paintings and the sculptures, that will allow the unique crisis of this individual death to take its place within the timeless order of the universe and also, within that kingdom by the Nile that had been fashioned in the image of that universal order.

These royal tombs, then, hold in them one of the first detailed maps of the universe man ever made; a description of the life that follows after life on earth and a description of all its ways and workings. The Valley of the Kings is one of the places where modern notions of sacredness were first examined and defined. In these caves was born something vital to all modern religion. Not specifically the Judaeo-Christian god – but part of the language, of the vocabulary, by which that god is understood. This is where part of our perception of deity itself was born. That is why it is so important to save these empty caverns, not solely for their beauty. These paintings and reliefs inside the tombs are the residue of people thinking deeply about life and death and sacredness.

Specifically, they deal with the passage from life to death and back again: between the sun going up and going down; between the king and his country dying and being reborn, just as fifteen hundred years later, and in a far and foreign country, Jesus Christ would rise up from the dead. On the walls of these tombs then, you see definitions of what it is to be dead, dead in a hundred ways of mind and body, and myriad speculations about the body and the mind as they are reborn. It is, of course, a spiritual definition of life that interests them, more than the valves of the heart or the functions of the spleen: that spiritual part of us that is specifically human. At the same time, it is also as if Christ's resurrection, as man and god, was described in tiny detail, as every nerve and every vein and all human sensibilities slowly regained vivacity and divinity. This then, is an intricate, an ancient definition of humanity; of mind and spirit and of the human body and its workings too, one of the most ancient visions of ourselves.

Today, these same great tombs and all their light and gentle paintings are amongst the most fragile monuments of ancient Egypt to have survived. Stand today, in one of the great vaulted tombs and look at this ancient work: these scenes are the products, the magical products, of just a few families, generations of people who lived in a little village not far from the Royal Valley and for two hundred years and more came to the tombs to work with a few copper chisels, stones, colours and brushes. The extraordinary transformations that these families wrought – these tombs were made with materials taken from the same desert landscape in which the royal tombs stand – delight an enormous throng of people every year.

There is much too, among these tombs, that tells their visitors about the persistence of delight, of skill and excellence and human dignity. Over the years, I have often stood in the heart of the simple tomb of Tutankhamun, beside him in his golden coffin. More than a million people each year now pass through that small space, and you may stand and watch the unending line shuffle in and peer through the glass at the golden face with its quiet smile. And you can see that sometimes, often unexpectedly, there arises among them the simple sensation of being in an ancient place with a young man who died three thousand years ago and more. There is a humanity here that reaches out to people. And the care of such things is part of being human.

Although these tombs are so very ancient, the names and lives of some of the artists who made them are known to us in quite surprising detail. Amenhotep, for example, whose name appears in a graffito among the decoration of the tomb of Ramesses VI, was a great painter who trained several of his sons to follow him in his profession. His large family included scribes and artists, foremen, labourers and stone cutters. When they were not working in the royal tombs, many family members also made some of the nobles' painted tombs and coffins that so delight us to this day. In the last great tombs of the Valley, it was Amenhotep's hand that drew the king's great Sun Boat on its starry journey through the underworld, drew the doors of the night, opening for the dead king, and drew the royal rebirth between the thighs of the great goddess. And here too, in the company of his sons, Amenhotep left a record of his own progress:

Year 9 [of the reign of Ramesses IX], 2 month of winter, day 14. On this day, the visit was made by the scribe Amenhotep and his son, the scribe and deputy draftsman Amennakht to see [the tomb]...[then] they went and looked at the hills.

And who would blame them? Like many other sites that ancient people chose, the hills around the Royal Valley are extraordinary in themselves. Walk down their pathways, white amidst the golden hills, and you walk with Amenhotep and his tomb makers. These are pharaohs' pathways.

A thousand years and more after him, some of the first Christian monks lived in these same Valleys, some of them within the royal tombs themselves, though carefully enough and without great damage to the ancient scenes. Thirty thousand years before them, Stone Age people had made arrowheads and axes on the hills above the tombs, and the remains of their flint factories are still there today, clusters of dark small stones dusted over the desert limestone. Many of the white paths cutting round and through the flints, though, were made in the time of the tomb makers, some of them chiselled from the natural hillside to make a wider path. The stones and staircases placed in these same paths were laid for the convenience of Amenhotep and his men.

This Valley, then, is not just an art gallery in tunnels, not just a mine for scholars in which to dig for dates and coffins, but a sacred landscape in itself. Imagine that you are standing in the cool morning air on top of the guardian mountain that overlooks the Valley of the Kings. From here, you can see the route taken by the funeral processions of the Theban kings. The officiating priests came to the royal funerary temples of western Thebes from their dwellings beside the state temples on the eastern bank, set amongst the huge city of Thebes, Homer's 'hundred-gated Thebes', one of the greatest urban centres of the ancient world, filled with the biggest temples man has ever made.

The western funerary temples served as the ministry of war and armaments, of the central taxing system too, and, at its centre, the embodiment of the ancient state surrounded by its officers and officials. In death, they gathered to ensure pharaoh's proper establishment in another world, an act that also established his successor on this earth and ensured the nation its accustomed prosperity.

The king was carried from the living Valley of the Nile, out from his palaces and temples so that his corpse could be made that of a god. As the sun set behind the western horizon, the pharaoh's mummy was carried in its flashing coffins on sledges over the cliffs and down into the Valley of the Kings to join the setting orb. All their lives, Amenhotep and his fellows, and their forefathers and successors, worked in this single desert valley, absorbed in the complex rituals of preparing a house for a god. The wide entrance passages of the tombs they made, that run so deep into the limestone cliffs, were called 'the corridors of the sun's path', and they were the entrances to the underworld, entrances that is, to those parts of creation that sustained Egypt and the Egyptians. The landscape here, then, is not a dramatic formal statement, either of art or faith. Nor were these tombs created to provide a baroque celebration of the rituals of a faith designed to entertain and overawe a mass of people. This is nothing less than the creation of a new universe of being, a universe that we still partly hold within us today; hold as a deep, deep metaphor of part of human thought and impulse.

In such landscapes as these, Egypt holds something of the metaphysics of the modern mind. And in their time, the ancient scribes knew this very well. Like whales and rainforests, such things belong to all of us, and they are also part of our collective responsibility. Unlike whales and rainforests though, tombs and monuments cannot reproduce or heal themselves.

Do you not know that Egypt is a copy of heaven, or rather, the very place on earth where the forces of heaven are balanced and ordered? Even more than that, if truth be told, Egypt is the temple of the entire world.

CHAPTER II

Rocks and Hard Places

TUTHMOSIS IV STARTS TO CRACK APART

When I first knew the Valley of the Kings in the 1960s, it seemed as if nothing had much changed there since ancient times. There were few enough visitors then, and many of the royal tombs had never been open to the public at all. If you wanted to see inside one of these closed tombs, you had to pay some local villagers to turn up in the Valley early in the morning with their farming tools, the heavy *fas*, the adzes that, as archaeological workmen, they also used in excavations. As the sunlight started to run down the sides of the Valley's hills, they would sing and dig at the ground, slowly uncovering the tomb steps as they cut lower and lower into the limestone dust and rubble, and their sons carried the debris away in baskets woven from palm fibres – those same rough baskets that the ancient monks who had lived in the Valley some fifteen hundred years before them had complained so cut their fingers as they wove them. After an hour or so of work, the top of an iron door would appear, then the remaining dirt was cleared away, and the dry stone wall that had been built against the bars to stop the loose dirt pouring into the tombs corridor was taken down. After your permission from the local Inspector of Antiquities was checked, a guard who worked in the Valley of the Kings would produce a circular key ring about nine inches across, bearing a variety of keys – the keys to all the tombs of the Valley. The tomb's door lock, covered in paper to protect it from the dirt in which it was buried, was carefully examined, the seal of the Chief Inspector of Antiquities attached between the tomb door and the door frame was broken and, finally, the door was swung open, grating and squeaking on the last of the limestone chippings and sending echoes deep into the dark tomb below. As you walked forward, you would feel a slow hot wind on your face, slightly scented with ancient cedar wood, filtering from the tomb.

Soon, you were scrambling down slippery stairways, these often badly damaged by the passage of the heavy stone sarcophagi into the tomb, and genuinely dangerous in the dark. Quite quickly you would be at the edge of the well, a deep pit dug by the tomb makers which trapped any flood waters that ran down from the tomb's entrance and usually situated, one observed, just at the point where the daylight finally ceased. Then, with a torch or a Coleman lamp, pumped and prodded by the foreman and delivered, roaring dangerously, into your hands at the tomb door with a few stern words about the light's fragility and expensiveness, you went down into the depths of the tomb. The well, a square and lethal pit, was often crossed by a plank with a wobbly rail attached to one side, though sometimes you had to bring a ladder with you and spend dangerous hours traversing the ancient hazard. On the other side, you would peer into the gloom and begin the slow descent into the Underworld. Usually, it was at that point that the paintings began. In the beam of your torch, you would see the glowing kings and gods upon the walls, rather as the ancient artists must have seen them as they worked in the small haloes of light provided by their oil lamps. After the well too, you would start to notice the fragments of ancient things: a robber's rope perhaps, tied around a column, its fibres now as fragile as a lamp mantle, but once strong enough to aid the ancient inspectors and robbers in their journeys through the tomb. And lying by a wall or posing dizzily upon a ledge, grimacing through dried and shrunken lips, you might have seen a mummy. Some of these were royal children, with the plaited lock of hair allowed only to princes. Some of them had blunt holes banged in their heads, others had their stomachs flapping open, slit cleanly with a sharp knife even before the embalmers' bitumen had set.

If at first the lowest rooms of the tombs seemed empty, a careful examination of the floor would soon bring to light a tiny residue of the wealth that once had been there. Small fragments of glistening blue faience would sparkle in the torchlight, pieces from royal bowls and dishes, scraps of those cross-armed servant figures so prized these days by auctioneers. There would be wooden splinters too, bits of the arms and legs of royal statues, and sometimes even planks of cedar and acacia with mortise slots in them, parts of the huge sledges that carried the sarcophagus into the tomb. And builders' beams too, which the tomb makers may have used and left behind them. And always, always pottery jars both smashed and whole. And cereals and linens too, once securely sealed inside their splendid whitewashed pots made in a shape so common that their descendents are used for olive oil right around the Mediterranean to this day. The heavy rounds of clay and linen lying everywhere throughout these tombs like half-deflated footballs were the remains of the sealings from those same jars, opened by the robbers, ancient and modern, in their passage through the tomb. This ancient debris, slivers of the past, ran right up to the side of the sarcophagi, great foursquare blocks of stone that rang like bells if you dared rap them with your knuckles. In one tomb, there was a room beside the sarcophagus filled with the butchered bones of four oxen, slaughtered and embalmed for the royal funeral and lying like a charnel house of giants. These rooms were always warm, and never frightening: echoing warehouses with little in them but the smell of spice. And paintings too; those paintings in their darkened galleries that seemed so rich, perhaps because of their exotic frames. But even today, under electric light, they seem just as fine as ever, though damaged now and stained by thoughtless sweaty hands.

In the earliest royal tombs – created before the business of making them had turned into an industry, in the days when the royal artists were drawn not from special gangs of royal tomb makers, but from the community of painters that learned their skills in private tombs – in those tombs especially, you found an unique art: an art of unusual solemnity for painters who normally took such great delight in drawing out the anecdotes of daily life, the harvesting, caring for the animals and all the activities of the people of the great estates. Here though, in rooms made only for the king and his gods, they painted only scenes of offering and the welcome of the gods for the dead monarch. Like the icon painters of

Byzantium who, when constrained in their subject matter by long tradition and a cruel court, invested the very lines and colour of simple ritual poses with an intensity and fire beyond all other painting in the land, the Theban artists lit these dark, dead royal tombs with glowing colours and a living line (see pl. 9).

It was in 1975 or thereabouts that I first noticed massive fractures in the walls of one of the very finest of these buried tombs, in the well of the tomb of Tuthmosis IV (see pl. 8, upper). I had not seen these cracks before, or perhaps I had just not noticed them. Perhaps before, the angle of my torch had not thrown up such large shadows on the tomb's wall: perhaps these cracks had broken open three thousand years before and I had walked past them, eager to get off that wobbly plank. I went to the library and to the scientific publication of the tomb. In fact, neither the walls of the well nor its fine paintings had ever before been photographed or, at any rate, such photographs as there were had not been published in a book. At that moment it was impossible to tell what, if anything, was going on.

The following year though, on returning to the tomb, things had changed. What had happened there was precisely what happens when fresh cracks appear on the walls of a modern house because the house has begun to move. The crack widens as the movement continues, the wall plaster covering the cracks continues to split until fragments of it start to fall. In 1976, I saw that a small piece of painted plaster which had been in place in the year before had fallen from the neck of a painted goddess right down into the well (see pl. 8, lower). Fresh splinters of rock had also dropped out of cracks in the burial chamber columns and onto the floor. And, it seemed to me, fresh water stains had appeared on the tomb walls.

RAMESSES I AND SETI, TOO

Later that year, quite unexpectedly, the ceiling of another tomb, that of Ramesses I, collapsed onto the royal sarcophagus, bruising the rose granite and damaging its funerary texts. The remainder of the tomb was quickly shored up with massive wooden beams and the local Antiquities officials shut the tomb to visitors. Then I noticed that in another tomb close by to it, in the dangerously ruined burial chamber of Ramesses III, more ceiling blocks had fallen too. At the same time, the ever-unfortunate tomb of Seti I close by, was also shedding further sections of its walls and ceilings. Something quite new seemed to be happening in these tombs: something was starting to devour them.

Now most local egyptologists knew of ancient earthquakes at Thebes, hieroglyphic texts in the temples often tell of rebuilding undertaken in their aftermath. But no-one at Thebes in living memory had seen or felt an earthquake large enough to cause these wall cracks. Perhaps then, it was the High Dam at Aswan that was causing the trouble? Completed as an act of Egypto-Soviet co-operation, the dam was no longer a favourite project of the western media. By 1977 the vast new lake behind the dam had been building up over a decade and was not yet at its full height. None the less, for several years there had been reports of a wide variety of plagues visiting Egypt: the demise of the sardine fleets, the salting of fields, the destruction of antiquities by ground-water seepage; all supposedly, the results of filling the High Dam. (It might be observed that today, since the African droughts and the drying of the Nile's headwaters, these disasters, if they ever really did result from the lake behind the dam, are seen as a small enough price to pay for the presence of this life-supporting reservoir.)

In 1976 at any rate, the threat to the royal tombs was genuine enough. Neither was this a case of 'Oh! these walls are very old and now they've cracked'. These walls had stood in the Valley for 3000 years and more without much change, then suddenly, disastrously, unannounced and unexpectedly, they cracked and fell. Geological specialists, experts in rocks and rock mechanics were required, first to discover what was happening and why, and then to provide some solutions. A friend found an answer close at hand. In between their survey work in the Egyptian desert, a team of oil prospectors from the Canoco/Marathon companies agreed to look at the Royal Valley and its tombs with me.

RAMESSES FLOODED

On 7 February 1977 a small group of geologists led by Coy C. Squyres came by taxi to the entrance of the Valley of the Kings, where I was waiting for them. Taller, more tanned and businesslike than the tourists who chattered all around them, the little group in battered hats and shorts and climbing boots seemed to me to be the natural successors of those nineteenth-century desert travellers. Successors, but far more practical; these men were professionals. In the event, they provided the Valley with three pioneering reports that would outline the basic problems of the tombs and suggest future programmes of research and conservation. First, we went down into the great ruined tomb of Ramesses II, to the right of the modern entrance of the Valley, down past the debris of ancient floods and desultory archaeology, down into the great burial chamber (see pls. 3, 4 & 5). Standing talking in that vast ruined burial vault, flashing their torches over its walls and floors piled high with the sand and boulders brought down by a succession of flash floods and churned by generations of archaeologists, they kicked the soft floor with their boots, grimaced at rock cracks, cursed the occasional blundering bat and scribbled in their notebooks. And as they talked, they showed me the geological mechanisms of that tomb's destruction.

The first of these, of course, was evident to anyone standing in the terribly scarred tomb. Ten or more flash floods had carried sand and flint and boulders down through its splendid painted chambers, and these unholy deluges had torn the paint and plaster from the walls and smashed the corners off rooms and doorways. But this immediate brutal attack had also brought with it another, subtler, source of damage. Underlying the limestone cliff in which the royal tomb was cut was a soft shale that was highly sensitive to water. Similar shales had long caused problems at oil rigs, they said, buckling drills and blocking pipes. When soaked in water, shale expands suddenly and with terrific force, and then it might even dissolve – put a piece into a glass of water and it hisses and seems almost to explode as it expands, disintegrates, and turns to mud. When the shale is lying under the limestone of a beautifully decorated tomb, as it was in the tomb of Ramesses II, even a trickle of water in the tomb could have a devastating effect, as the soaked shale expands and heaves. As we talked together in Ramesses' burial chamber, I saw that we were standing on a stratum of this soft springy shale and looking up at broken limestone vaults and walls; the great tomb was bedded on something almost as volatile as soluble Aspirin.

When the floods had entered Ramesses II's tomb then, they had smashed down through the limestone corridors and soaked straight into the soft shale of the burial chamber floor. Under the tremendous pressure of its expansion – thousands upon thousands of pounds of pressure – the shale pushed the limestone walls and columns of the tomb up into the mountain overhead and they had cracked and shattered like the windscreen of a car.

Like a windscreen though, at first the tomb had roughly kept its shape and form, held by the pressure exerted by the shale. But then, as the shale dried over the following years, it slowly sank back to its previous position. So the pressure on the walls and columns was relaxed and slowly, year after year, decade after decade, piece by piece, the shattered tomb began to fall. That, then, is why huge decorated fragments of walls and columns are usually to be found lying on top of, rather than underneath, the dried-out flood debris in such damaged tombs; the splintered stone had not fallen for years, perhaps even centuries after the destroying floods had come and gone.

The only floods that were recorded as entering the tomb of Ramesses II were the very last, in 1913 and 1914. Though these floods had run through the Valley of the Kings since long before the time of the pharaohs – in earlier geologic epochs, the entire Valley had been shaped by them – modern accounts of these terrifying events were few and far between. On 25 October 1918, however, while sitting on the veranda of his house by the entrance to the Valley of the Kings, Howard Carter saw one of these devastating occurrences and, in a letter to his patron, Lord Carnarvon, he wrote an account of what he saw:

Towards the sunset, as the desert cooled, there was a great storm in the North West. No rain fell in the Valley [of the Kings], but from all the washes that ran down from the Theban Hills there was a torrent which cut furrows four feet deep and rolled stones as big as two feet across. The locals were unable to ford the floods when returning from their work in the fields as the area was a vast lake. Yet no rain fell. Then, later, came a heavy downpour, which was the edge of the storm whose centre had been approximately ten miles back in the hills. There was a great roar, and a wall of water came out of the Valley smashing through the village and the local graveyard so that bodies were floating in the Nile, killing cows and even killing some people.

With such experience as this, it is not surprising that in 1922, before he started the work of clearing the treasures from Tutankhamun's tomb, Carter built a breakwater in the valley because he was worried about the potential flooding of his newly opened tomb. Years earlier, he had built another breakwater behind the expedition house of the Valley of the Kings, so that he could sleep peacefully in his bed at night.

The evidence of the residue that they left, deposits of fine sand and light grey mud right though the tomb, shows that the 1913-14 floods that ran into the tomb of Ramesses II were comparatively light streams of water. At the time of the last flood, Harry Burton, the fine photographer who later worked with Carter documenting Tutankhamun's tomb, was himself excavating in the Valley of the Kings and was both alarmed and intrigued by these gentle streams running into the great tomb. Where on earth was all this water going?

Within a week or two, he and his workmen had burrowed down through the damp debris of earlier floods and had arrived in the lowest sections of the tomb. Here, he notes in his records, the burial chamber was very hot and humid, so hot in fact, that he recorded its temperature – around 90° Fahrenheit – in his notebooks; this was the first time such data had been collected in the Valley of the Kings. Geologists affirm that this rise in temperature is a product of a chemical reaction that often occurs when shale is soaked with water, a reaction that was noticed in 1817 when Europeans had first entered the tomb of Seti I and the flood waters had followed them. As the redoubtable Mrs Belzoni remembered:

on the 11th of December [1817]...A heavy rain, accompanied with thunder and lightening, commenced an hour after sunset, and continued the whole of the night: it poured in torrents. My mattress and coverings were wet through...it came pouring from the mountains through the lands into the Nile on each side for several days after. I arrived at Luxor on the 16th... crossed the Nile, and took up my residence at Beban el Malook [the Valley of the Kings]. The men left to guard the tomb...informed me of the heavy rain they had experienced on the night I mentioned, and, in spite of all their efforts, they could not prevent the water entering the tomb; it had carried in a great deal of mud, and, on account of the great heat, and the steam arising from the damp, made some of the walls crack, and some pieces had fallen. On hearing this I went into the tomb, and the only thing we could do was to order a number of boys to take the damp earth away...

Nearly a century on, Harry Burton and his men were employing the same remedy in the tomb of Ramesses II, and with the same results. As his men dug out the sand and rocks, the tomb began to fall around them. The ceilings were particularly precarious: 'great pieces of the roof had to be pulled down' is a common note in his notebooks. Despite placing beams in the tomb, Burton and his men felt unsafe. As far as antiquities were concerned, the pickings had been decidedly thin; realizing that they were doing more harm than good, Burton left the tomb to dry out by itself.

In 1977 though, Burton's efforts had not escaped the quick eyes of the six geologists. 'The debris in some of the chambers,' Squyres noted later in his report, 'had numerous pick marks suggesting that the sediment was wet when the tomb was excavated.' As we left the tomb, they pointed out to me that Burton's wooden buttresses, pit props balanced on piles of flood debris, would have saved neither him nor us from injury had the ceilings begun to fall. They also pointed out to me that although, to the casual visitor, the tomb might seem bone dry, we had spent half an hour or more amongst its sand and dirt and almost none of it had been kicked up into the air. This, they felt, was because the tomb itself was still quite humid. If this were so, of course, it was still drying from the floods of more than sixty years before. And if it was still drying, the rocks of the tomb would still be moving.

RAMESSES FAULTED

Before that day was over, we had visited half a dozen royal tombs. I started to realize that many of the tombs were cut to a depth where the floors of the limestone burial chambers just met the shale stratum that lay beneath. Clearly the ancient tomb makers realized the weakness of the underlying shale. Where the builders had not reached the shale, the geologists pointed out to me, the architecture of the tomb was fairly sound – and this was usually seen in the tombs in the higher sections of the Valley, that stand some 20 and 30 metres above the shale. The tombs at the centre of the Valley however, like that of Ramesses II, were close to the shale and had suffered terrible damage.

As we stood under the huge creaking burial vault of Ramesses III, another of the tombs close to the shale, the roof above seemed to be so loose that a sneeze or a stamp of the foot might send down limestone slabs large enough to kill us. One of the geologists, John Harms, pointed out to me that the mud that covered the chamber's floor bore on its surface the typical polygonal cracks which occur when mud dries out and shrinks. He noticed too that on this same mud there were imprints of modern shoes, and whispered that this flood had been recent, a fact that fitted perfectly with my knowledge of the history of the tomb. In 1817 an agent of the British Consul in Egypt removed the royal sarcophagus from the tomb and the lid had been turned over and broken by the waters of a flash flood just as his workmen were carrying it out of the Valley. Clearly, the deep, flat and undisturbed mud lying in the tomb's burial chamber had been deposited in the tomb at some time after that date, that is, in the epoch of the modern shoe.

Unlike most of the Valley's tombs, Ramesses III's had never been hidden from view in all of its long history. Since the first days of European exploration, it had been one of the Valley's most famous monuments, and certainly it had not always had this bare wrecked cavern of a burial chamber, but a fine vaulted room decorated with the scenes of pharaoh's journey through the hours of the night. Above all, though, the tomb of Ramesses III had been famed for its pretty pictures of palace life; of royal furniture and food and stores and sailing boats and blind musicians. Coloured copies of the tomb's paintings appear in all the great scholarly publications of the nineteenth century. Quite suddenly though, in 1910, a guide book paints a very different picture of the tomb. After a lengthy and enthusiastic account of its upper rooms, it concludes abruptly: 'The remaining chambers are now closed to the public. The scenes are much damaged, and they are not of great interest.' Standing in the burial chamber, I could see what had happened. A long rock fault, cutting at an acute angle through the chamber's left wall, had allowed huge amounts of water and fine sand to flood the room. The eroded wall was standing precariously, block on block like a gigantic strainer, awaiting the waters of the next desert storm to percolate through it. The tail of sand that had been conducted into the chamber during the last vast flood still lay around its base.

The tomb had flooded then, and flooded badly, and collapsed. But, unlike the tomb of Ramesses II, the water here had not entered through the door; the famous upper sections of the tomb with all their gaudy decorations were as bright as ever. Clearly no water had passed that way. In the lower sections of the tomb, though, the decoration had all but disappeared. The tomb had flooded from the bottom up; the tide of the flood's full extent is clearly marked by a sharp edge of decay in the last corridors before the lowest chambers of the tomb. At a time around the turn of the century then, you could have walked through the long dry upper corridors of the tomb and fetched up at the edge of a rectangular pool of water that was lapping at the stairs. Had you dived into this unpromising pool, you could have swum through the lower corridors, and gathered your breath in the vault of the burial chamber which would have been serving as an airlock!

Seti excavated

At first, the six geologists were puzzled when they went into the tomb of Seti I, which still bore in its burial chamber the white scars of recent rock falls from its great astronomical ceiling. I told them that the tomb had flooded only once, in 1817; they told me that the patterns of the cracks threatening the burial chamber, long straggling shivers running right through the beautiful painted relief, were not of a type made by upwards pressure from the shale below. This, then, was not the primary water damage that they had seen in other tombs. For the first time, one of the geologists raised the possibility of a sudden shaking of the tomb – a recent earthquake, perhaps, or blasting. I knew there were no records of such events here in modern times, but, certainly, this did not preclude the possibility. And of course, there were those ancient restoration texts in Karnak Temple across the river, recording the pious rebuilding of some of the temple doorways in Ptolemaic times, after massive earthquakes had shaken the very houses of the gods themselves.

However, when I told the geologists about Sheik Ali's excavations seventeen years previously, a more immediate explanation presented itself. 'The area where these cracks are most visible,' John Harms wrote later in his report, 'is above and adjacent to the tunnel excavated by Sheik Ali Abd er Rassul in the late 1950s. Subsidence damage related to this shaft may be responsible for the fairly recent damage, and might be alleviated by placing beams and jacks in that tunnel.'

The shale of the burial chamber floor seemed to be shrinking away from its limestone walls as it lost its humidity after the Sheik's excavations had driven open the tunnel beneath and let in the dry desert air. But other aspects of the damage still seemed difficult to explain in terms of the Sheik's assault upon the tomb. Noting that tourists had greatly damaged the walls of Seti I's tomb by touching and scratching them, one of the geologists suggested that the very breathings of visitors in these tombs would have great effect upon the levels of humidity in them and, possibly therefore, upon the water-sensitive rock in which they had been cut. All this clearly needed further investigation, they said, and they recommended a geological survey of the Valley and laboratory testing of both its limestone and its shale.

RAMESSES FALLEN

After Seti's sad tomb, we went next door, to the equally unfortunate tomb of Ramesses I which had collapsed just two years earlier. Before the geologists went down to the burial chamber, I tiptoed through it, picking up a dozen and more tiny fragments of the wall paintings which had fallen to the floor. Unfortunately, it was too late to save a large slab of loosened plaster by the doorway which, old photographs showed, had borne a cartouche, with splendid painted hieroglyphs of the king's name within it. The two-foot long slab had long gone – now perhaps it resides in a museum basement in Europe or America, maturing like old wine until it can be brought back into the light again without scandal (see pl. 7, lower).

Until these cracks and robberies, this little tomb had been quite perfect – just as bright as in the first days of the painting of its decorations, which had been hurried along to receive the mummy of the elderly but short-reigned king. Once down in the royal burial chamber, the geologists dodged in and out and all around the scaffolding surrounding the sarcophagus (see pl. 6), pausing only to write in their notebooks. Later, sipping beers in the lavish granite Rest House which then stood at the Valley's centre, they promised me their individual reports. Even at that time though, John Harms said that he thought that the rise in the water table seemed to be an unlikely ingredient in either the deterioration of the temples or the tombs. (Before they arrived at the Valley that morning, they had examined some of the Theban temples, looking unsuccessfully for evidence of the much publicized effects of the High Dam.) On one thing all of them were agreed: a major multinational effort was required if the deterioration in the royal tombs was to be slowed to acceptable proportions. And time was pressing; as Coy Squyres later wrote in his report, 'If something is not done soon, many of the monuments of Thebes will just be a memory'.

The three geological reports arrived within the month. Most of the problems in the royal tombs, they had concluded, seemed to be related to water. In their account of individual tombs, they continually commented upon the relationship of water and humidity to cracking and collapsing. 'Several tombs show evidence of cata-strophic flooding, either in Pharaonic times or much more recently. This flooding can have a devastating structural effect, especially where tomb floors reach the level of the shale beds which, by virtue of clay content, can change volume and cause heaving. The problem is aggravated where the tomb is then opened and dried, allowing a subsequent shrinking and subsi-dence.'

Though at that time there was little interest among egyptolo-gists in these huge ruined tombs, the survey geologists also specif-ically warned future intending excavators: 'A lot of damage occurred during the evacuation [excavation] of tombs especially by taking out wet flood debris. Careful work by thoughtful archaeol-ogists would stop this.' In 1992, with several new excavations underway in recently flooded tombs in the Valley of the Kings, I telephoned John Harms and told him what was going on and he was sufficiently alarmed immediately to volunteer to come and inspect the tombs again, and advised me to contact other mem-bers of the first surveying party.

In 1977, those first reports had necessarily been tentative in tone. As scientists, the geologists required accurate statistics to reach beyond impressions gained from long experience. In con-sequence of this, they wrote that the rock movements 'might' have been caused by water; that Sheik Ali's excavations 'may' have been responsible for damage in Seti's tomb, and so on. Nat-urally, they recommended an extensive programme of further investigation. Laboratory tests should be performed upon the limestone and the shale, they said; maps should be drawn to establish the pattern of the flood waters passing through the Val-ley, this as a first stage of preventing the floods from penetrating the tombs again. Detailed studies of the faults and rock cracks in the valley should be made, and equipment installed in the tombs to measure rock movement and humidity. First and most funda-mental of all, however, a basic geological survey of the area was needed. For in all its history, the Valley of the Kings – indeed the whole vast area of ancient Thebes – had never been geologically surveyed in detail.

Things go better

In 1977, generously funded by the Coca Cola Company of Atlanta, Georgia, a start was made on the next stage of the work. After some preliminary laboratory testing on samples of limestone and shale from the Valley and its tombs, Professor Garniss Curtis of the Faculty of Earth Sciences at University of California, Berkeley, established that changing humidity levels were apparently not hazardous to the limestone tomb walls as the Canoco/Marathon team had hypothesized: 'The data suggests, but it would take more testing to prove definitely, that large changes in atmospheric humidity in the tombs have little effect on the marly limestones in the walls and ceilings. Liquid water, however, has a very deleterious effect.'

So far, so good. But then Curtis also re-established the long-neglected fact that it was not only the shale that was dangerously affected by water, but that the limestone was also vulnerable, as Belzoni's expedition had found in 1817, in the tomb of Seti I:

While I was absent up the Nile it happened to rain; the water, finding the entrance [of Seti I] open, ran into the tomb, and though not much, was enough to occasion some damage to some of the figures. The dryness of the calcareous stone, which is more like lime itself than raw stone, absorbed the dampness, and consequently cracked in many places, particularly in the angles of the pillars on the doorways, etc.; and in one of the rooms there was a piece of stone detached, containing the upper part of three figures; and in another chamber, was a figure, which fortunately fell without much injury; though broken in three pieces I saved it from farther destruction. I was not a little vexed to see such a thing happen. The damage done at that time was inconsiderable in a place of such extent; but I fear, that in the course of a few years it will become much worse; and I am persuaded, that the damp in the rainy days has caused as much damage in the tombs as has been occasioned in any other way.

With somewhat greater brevity, Professor Curtis summed up his account of this same phenomenon by noting that 'the absorption and expansion properties of the limestone have great importance in planning for the future preservation of the tombs; for while it was known that expansion of the Esna Shale when wet had caused very extensive damage in those tombs that penetrate the shale, it was not known that the limestone also expanded when wet, with consequent change'.

This ill-wind blew some good towards the tombs, however. The phenomenon of the expansion of water-soaked limestone provided the explanation for the mechanism by which water had penetrated and flooded the Valley's tombs from water-bearing rock faults. If even small quantities of rain water entered a tiny crack, commented Curtis, 'absorption causes the limestone to swell, developing enormous pressures parallel to the ground surface. The limestone expands vertically also, but there is no resistance in this direction, and it can move upward freely. Laterally, however, it cannot move, so it deforms slightly or "creeps" down-slope. When the water dries out again, the limestone contracts, leaving a joint that is now opened slightly. The next rain can now penetrate into the joint still further and the joint can hold more water. The process continues with every rain, gradually opening the joint further and further and deeper and deeper. The time necessary to develop large openings in these joints must be tens of thousands of years... the importance of this mechanism to the royal tombs is that many joints occur directly above the tombs and are undoubtedly permitting water to penetrate deeply enough to dampen the wall surfaces of the tombs, with consequent swelling and displacement of large blocks of limestone and spalling of the walls themselves. I believe this is the case in the tombs of Seti I and Ramesses I as in others.'

Now the survey seemed to be getting somewhere, especially when Curtis was also able specifically to discount earthquakes and other seismic activity as a factor in the tomb's recent cracking and collapses. For the first time, he identified the two main rock faults in the Valley, elements basic to the shape and drainage of the entire region.

Careful examination of the shining bands of calcite crystal in these two faults, exposed by the ancient tomb cutters working deep inside the tombs, showed that there had been no seismic activity in the Valley of the Kings for a very long time. These bright water-deposited crystals which filled and blocked the two main faults had neither moved nor shattered since the time of their deposition: the

brisk chisel cuts of the ancient quarrymen running across the calcite and the limestone lying together showed that here at least,
where they were exposed, none of the interfaces of these two great
faults had moved since the royal tombs were made.

BUT STILL, A CENTRAL MYSTERY

Though our research had solved the mystery of the mechanisms
of deterioration and destruction in the royal tombs, it still had not
solved the problem that had raised these questions in the first
place: why was it that so many of the royal tombs had suddenly
began to crack and twist in the 1970s?

Those intact calcite crystals showed that there had been no
recent earthquakes in the Valley; rock tests showed that no amount
of tourists breathing on the ancient walls would bring them down.
Similarly, vibrations from the buses and coaches bringing tourists
to the Valley that might have accelerated damage in tombs close to
the road could hardly cause damage in tombs like Tuthmosis IV
that were half a mile away and high up on the mountainside.
Similarly, the only excavation to have taken place in the Valley of
the Kings since the opening of Tutankhamun's tomb was Sheik
Ali's disastrous dig, and that could hardly have caused the rash of
disasters that were taking place across the Valley. What, then, was
there left to consider? Though the surveys had isolated the general
motors of change, they had not described any one specific recent
driver. What was necessary was to isolate a brand new factor in
the desert landscape, something introduced into it in the decades
before the recent spate of damage had started to occur.

In the event, there had been just one new factor introduced into
the royal Valley: the Rest House at the Valley's centre with its café
and rest rooms, built in the first years after the Revolution by an
optimistic government planning for an enlarging tourist trade. The
sewage from this Rest House ran underground, encased in concrete in a single large-bore sewage pipe, right through the Valley's
centre. As it passed the famous tombs close by, it seemed secure
enough, but outside this immediate area it emptied into a closed
concrete septic tank.

Now, this tank was something of a mystery, a reversed version of the widow's cruse. For though it was constantly filled with liquid from the Rest House, it was hardly ever emptied. Over the years, untold amounts of water must have leaked down into the shale which, as our geological survey had shown us, ran right across the Valley landscape at an elevation of around 150 metres – that is, some thirty feet beneath the bottom of the concrete tank. As anyone may see, the entire landscape of the Valley is fractured and fissured by large cracks and faults which, our research had told us, were constantly enlarged by desert rains. Any of these conduits could have been taking the sewage water down into the shale. This then seemed to be the wild card, the single new factor in the ecology of the Royal Valley, the only visible explanation of the sudden heaving and moving of rocks right around the valley that had damaged so many of its tombs. For if large amounts of water from the sewage system had soaked into the shale stratum, this would cause immense pressure among the loosely faulted natural rock formations of the Valley. The situation of the Valley and its tombs would then resemble the fragments of a smashed tile lying on a soaked and drying sponge; the slow heaving and contraction of the fractured architecture of the tombs reflecting the slightest changes in underground humidity.

THE GREAT LESSON

One thing was sure: major monuments were suffering and no chances needed to be taken – this unfortunate cess pit should be shut. The situation was explained to the local Government Antiquities officials who had independently been worried about the effects of sewage water in the Valley. Letters were drafted and, from the head offices of the EAO in Cairo, orders were sent to the hotel chain that operated the Rest House, requiring them to close it down. Today, the Rest House has been remade with an attendant coach park and greatly improved facilities a mile down valley from the tombs, and in its old place stands a simple and elegant sun shelter.

At last, it seemed that the immediate problems of the Valley had been solved. Though the underlying shale probably held thousands of gallons of water, it was well sealed in the rock, with only rock faults and cracks to permit evaporation over many years. The royal tombs had always been subjected to such slow processes of movement since the days that they were made – in some tombs, you can even see some of the adjustments and repairs made by the ancient quarrymen and masons as the natural limestone they were cutting dried and fractured as it was first exposed to air. The Valley's natural rocks and all its tombs are dynamic structures, just as they have always been. Now, after the closure of the cess pit, this fresh ferocious onslaught of water and humidity had been checked. Such damage as might occur in the future would be slow and might be anticipated and controlled.

One thing was certain: the Valley of the Kings and all its tombs were on a knife's edge. Any violent changes, floods and storms and human activities – the opening up of previously sealed tombs, building cafés or making archaeological clearances across the Valley floor – could have immediate and damaging effects upon the royal tombs.

The tomb of Seti, for example, had only flooded once in modern times, and only, apparently, to a depth of a few feet, and that as long ago as 1817. Thirty years ago, Sheik Ali excavated in the tomb: the damage he promoted continues to this day. More than anywhere else, it is in places like the tomb of Seti I that you can really appreciate the lengths of time it takes for things to happen in the Valley of the Kings: the time it takes for water and humidity to work their way through the rock and the tombs; the time that elapses between cause and effect.

CHAPTER III

Digging in the Dark

ARCHAEOLOGISTS AT WORK, AGAIN

To my apprehension and great amazement, in the late 1980s archaeologists started to dig again in the Valley of the Kings. By 1990, no less than four expeditions were digging in the tombs around the head of the Valley; more were planned to follow them and I was writing a warning paper about their work, to be read at the International Congress of Egyptology in Turin in 1991.

A series of physical surveys of the Valley of the Kings were conducted during 1977–9...These surveys described the basic mechanisms of the geological processes that continue to damage and destroy these great monuments, and criteria were established to monitor and control them. However, recent archaeological activity in the Valley shows very little awareness of this work. Indeed, several current and projected enterprises will actually accelerate and multiply rates of destruction in the royal tombs beyond anything yet seen... the present situation of the Valley and its tombs resembles the fragments of a smashed tile on a drying sponge; the closing of the cess pit and the opening and drying of any tombs such as KV 5, that are connected to it [one of the tombs under excavation], requires precise monitoring throughout large sections of the Valley and its tombs...similarly, rapid desiccation prompted by the excavation of hard packed flood debris from a tomb – the clearance for example, of tombs such as those of Bay [also under excavation] or Amenmesse or Ramesses II [projected for excavation] – not only threatens the collapse of the tomb under excavation but others in the vicinity, and this for decades after...Of the 75 known tombs in the Valley of the Kings, more than half are only partially excavated and one third are completely lost from view.

58

Attractive, famous and convenient, it is hardly surprising that the Valley has once again become a favoured site for small scale egyptological field work. But if future generations are to regard this renewed activity as anything more than the exploitation of ancient monuments in the name of science, the basic requirements of modern conservation must be met.

The first reaction I encountered at the conference was brusque: I was told that, if I had seen the amounts of 'conservation' that one of these expeditions had performed, I would not have written as I did. I had not even bothered to go to the Valley and look for myself, they said – and that was true enough! Similarly, a small report of my paper in the popular archaeology magazine *K.M.T.*, written by the wife of one of the new excavators, also suggested that I was somewhat out of date:

A claim by popular British author and video personality John Romer that the Valley of the Kings is about to cave in has been discounted by antiquities sources here [written from Cairo]. Romer based his dire prediction on a geological survey conducted in the Theban royal necropolis fourteen years ago.

The item concluded by saying that I had made 'an emotional plea' for 'massive and immediate restoration efforts' to be 'focused on the Valley'. Though it did occur to me that perhaps the geology of the desert sometimes took more than fourteen years to go out of date, perhaps it was true that, although I had stated the general principle, I did not know exactly what was going on in particular in these new excavations. So I went back to the Valley of the Kings again to see what was happening on the ground. The reality proved to be more disquieting than I had ever imagined. Here was no brave new archaeology, just more of the same....

KINGS' VALLEY 5

Just a short distance away from the old cess pit, hidden now behind a bright row of souvenir stalls, I found the doorway of a tomb whose re-opening had been reported in the international press. This tomb, called simply Kings' Valley 5 (= KV 5), was long known to have been a family tomb of the time of Ramesses II.

Now, the tomb's re-openers had established that it was the tomb of at least two of that King's princely sons; Ramesses, his texts inform us, had more than a hundred such offspring.

The nineteenth-century plans of the tomb already showed that KV 5 was of regal size – large enough, indeed, to hold all the King's children. Early visitors reported that, like Ramesses II's own tomb just under fifty metres away, it was ruined and half-full of flood debris. The sketch plans published by its American re-openers, a part of a project originally fielded by the University of California at Berkeley, bore out the early observations. From calculations based on these plans, it is probable that there are more than fifteen hundred tons of flood debris inside this tomb, though this is a conservative estimate based on known rooms. The tomb itself might hold yet more surprises; the expedition's Director, Professor Kent R. Weeks of the American University in Cairo, wrote in his 1992 report upon his activities at the tomb that, 'attempts to probe beyond doorways of presently accessible chambers have already indicated that the tomb continues on in several different directions for not inconsiderable distances'.

Further reading of the report helped solve a considerable mystery that dated from the days of the geological surveys. As the Professor recounts: 'When we removed a portion of the debris blocking the tomb's doorway, we were met by a rush of hot, moist air, the result of leaks in the sewer pipe.' So this was where the water from the cess pit had been going for all those years! During our earlier survey work we had often theorized that this unfortunate tomb might well be doing second duty as a septic tank and be filled with sewer water and destruction; now we knew for sure. Weeks further commented that, 'This moisture had caused significant deterioration of the wall surfaces, and indicated that the clearing of the initial chambers would have to be accompanied by a slow and especially meticulous process of cleaning, conservation, and recording'. He continued,

the air in the tomb on this first look-see was so bad that we were able to remain inside the tomb for only a few minutes before we had to return to the entrance. When we left the tomb, we blocked the doorway with stones, not sand, so that the interior air quality could slowly improve before we conducted further work. Six months later, we returned to KV 5 with a small work force....

Amazingly enough, despite the experiences of Mr and Mrs Belzoni, of Harry Burton, Howard Carter, Sheik Ali and all the rest (see Ch.1, pp 27–8, and Ch.2), this expedition had aired out the tomb while it was still soaked with water, then proceeded to remove flood debris from inside its first chamber, thus depriving the shrinking stone of its physical support and exposing it further to the drying desert air. In a Valley where catastrophic damage had occurred in other tombs after centuries and more of gradual drying, six months seemed to me to be a perilously short period of time to allow before carrying out such a clearance of debris.

It occurred to me that possibly the excavators were unaware of the special perils connected with clearing flooded tombs in the particular environment of the Valley of the Kings. Certainly they were aware of the effects of flooding: 'the most substantial damage was done to the first two chambers by the leaking sewer pipe...but there also was damage from a longer term problem: flash floods...' However, their account of the mechanisms of damage in parts of the tomb they are excavating largely discounts even that, Weeks remarking that, in the 1820s,

Burton [James Burton, an early egyptologist] commented on the deep, water borne fill with which KV 5 was packed, and Lane referred to large areas of the ceiling that had collapsed into the chambers, in part because of this flooding.

This 'in part', which is not Lane's own qualification, seems to me, if I understand him correctly, to refer to Weeks's hypothesis that 'serious structural damage' in sections of the tomb was the result of vibrations caused by tourist coach traffic; traffic which – unlike the excavations – has now ceased.

However this may be, the visits of Hay and Lane to the ruined tomb took place long before the invention of the internal combustion engine and, even in their time, damage to the tomb was extensive and considerable. Perhaps the proximity of vibrating tour buses – which Weeks, quite erroneously, describes as passing above some of the tomb's chambers – was the straw that finally broke the ruined tomb. But no buses have ever visited the vicinity of the tombs of Seti I or Ramesses III, and today their walls and ceilings are moving and heaving because of the processes of desiccation – processes that in Seti I's case have been dangerously accelerated precisely by the excavation of flood debris from inside the tomb.

No doubt, more stone will also fall in KV 5 in the near future, as the limestone continues to dry. The expedition has already found it necessary to install ceiling props in the first chambers of the unfortunate tomb. In its entirety, KV 5 is very large. It has been the recipient of an unknown quantity of soiled water over a period of two to three decades. Lying about thirty feet under the entrance doorway, it is probable that the shale stratum of the Valley is physically exposed in the lower sections of the tomb, as was the custom of the tomb makers in the period in which the tomb was made. At all events, the rock in which the tomb is cut is so fissured that, for safety's sake if not for common sense, we must assume that the water has found its way down to the underlying shale. If large amounts of debris are removed, with the consequent alteration of the humidity levels in the tomb, the ensuing rock shrinkages and falls could be massive. It is not impossible, for example, that the hill in which the tomb is cut would itself collapse. Unlike the tomb of Ramesses II nearby, which runs down under the valley's cliffs, KV 5 was cut into a small hill at the centre of the Valley.

Nor is this all. The pattern of rock faults in this hill above the tomb prompts further alarm, not simply concerning the fate of KV 5 itself, but the splendid painted monuments at the heart of the Valley – the tombs of Tutankhamun, of Ramesses VI and Ramesses IX – which also join this same system of cracks and faults. This system is part of a series of parallel slip faults that run right across the hill of KV 5 towards the centre of the Valley where, in the vicinity of the great tomb of Ramesses VI, they meet another, similar set of parallel faults. You can trace the diamond patterns that this union has made across the floors and ceilings of that tomb. These faults that take in KV 5 also pass through the tomb of Tutankhamun, also at the centre of the Valley, and these are known to carry water in them. In January 1907, as the archaeologist Gaston Maspero felt beneath the rotted, golden coffin of a queen in another tomb,

KV 55, that also sits upon these same rock faults, he suddenly pulled out his hands exclaiming that he had 'found something never before seen in a tomb in Egypt'. To his amazement, and to that of the other excavators, his hands were dripping wet. Today, in this same tomb, not twenty yards from Tutankhamun's, tufts of salt, like blobs of icing on a birthday cake, are growing from the wall where the rock fault crosses the tomb; they bear testimony to that old leak when the tomb's floor was wet and humidity was high.

Clearly, the unfortunate KV 5 is at the centre of a system of drainage and drying in the Valley and we should, in all due caution, assume at the centre, too, of the greatest disturbances the Valley of the Kings has seen since the floods of 1918. The 1991 water leak in the roof of Tutankhamun's tomb (see pp. 23 ff.) was a grim reminder that the rocks in this series of faults are still moving, for it was heaving rock that, for the first time in thousands of years, caused the old crystal-bound rock fault in the tomb to open and let the rain water pass. Similarly, between December 1991 and July 1993, on three separate visits to the Valley, several large cracks were observed to have appeared in the recent restoration work in the first corridors of the great painted tomb of Ramesses IX. The front of this tomb, close to KV 5, is on the move and, situated in the same system of rock faults, serves once again to underline the fragility and vulnerability of this entire area at the heart of the Royal Valley.

I am surprised that in his report, Professor Weeks appears to minimize the effects of water damage and desiccation. I regard these factors as fundamental to the planning of work close to some of the finest and most celebrated monuments to have survived from ancient Egypt. Doubtless, some interesting historical information will be gained from the excavation of KV 5. However, if the fabric of the tomb is to be risked by its full excavation and such vast quantities of flood debris removed, then to safeguard the other nearby tombs, the work should properly be accompanied by extensive rock tests and crack surveys, and the installation of a variety of gauges in a dozen tombs and more. And, experience has taught us, these monitoring devices should be maintained and inspected for decades to come.

Plate 1. In the evening's afterglow, deserted by visitors, the Valley of the Kings returns to something like its ancient reality. Between 1500 and 1000 BC, the world's most powerful monarchs were buried here. Tutankhamun lies at the Valley's centre; the entrance to his tomb is inside the walled rectangle at the photograph's lower left.

Plate 2 (upper). The lintel above the entrance of the tomb of King Ramesses X, drawn in the 1820s by an artist of Champollion's expedition.

Plate 2 (lower). The same scene in 1979. Flash floods have washed away both paint and plaster. Beyond this doorway, the entire tomb is solidly blocked with flood debris.

Plate 3. The entrance corridor of the tomb of Ramesses II, scoured by water and half-filled with flood debris. The boxes and baskets hold desultory finds from excavations conducted in 1914.

Plate 4. Deep down in the tomb of Ramesses II, one walks between high walls of flood debris, a passageway cut by archaeologists on their way to the royal burial chamber below. Horizontal bands of sand and stone in the debris are witness to the deposits of successive floods. More than ten separate floodings have been counted in the tomb.

Plate 5. The burial chamber of Ramesses II, heaped with the debris of the archaeologists' unsuccessful attempts to find the royal burial. Flood waters have almost destroyed the wall reliefs. The long horizontal crack to the right of the doorway is typical of damage caused by the shrinking shale as it dries and leaves the limestone above it unsupported. Today, Ramesses's tomb stands like a natural cavern.

Plate 6. In the 1970s, fresh cracks suddenly appeared in several tombs in the Valley of the Kings. In the jewel-like burial chamber of King Ramesses I, slabs of rock fell from the ceiling onto the royal sarcophagus, and the roof had to be supported against further falls with massive wooden beams.

Plate 7 (upper). Many of the fresh cracks in the tomb of Ramesses I, largely hidden behind the plaster and the painting of the tomb decoration, appeared at first to be insignificant. In the photograph, one of these cracks starts by the upper part of the door jamb, runs through the coils of the snake and then downwards, into the banded borders and black dado to the floor. Their effect, however, was dramatic; by 1977 small fragments of the ancient paintings were littering the tomb's floor.

Plate 7 (lower). Some sections of the burial chamber's walls became so loose that a piece of plaster bearing a beautifully painted royal name (right of the doorway) was pulled off by an unknown visitor and has never been seen again.

The tomb of the Chancellor

During that first investigative trip in December 1991, I came across an excavation that was still underway. Just three hundred yards up the Valley from the sad entrance of KV 5, a procession of workmen was carrying flood debris from the tomb of Chancellor Bay, a small but infinitely intriguing monument that previously had been stopped as tight as a cork by ancient flood debris. Egyptologists had speculated upon this unusual tomb for a long time. Now it was possible to see if the tantalizing traces of decoration and inscription that were visible around the doorway extended further down into the tomb. A brand-new part of the Valley's history was emerging in front of my eyes!

As I looked at the workmen though, I realized with horror that the flood debris they were carrying from the tomb was wet, and you may see this quite clearly in the photograph (see pl. 15). The sand and chippings that had been carried from the excavation at the bottom of the tomb were darker in colour than the rest of the tip. Almost as soon as the debris was laid out in the sunlight though, it quickly dried and turned a lighter shade. This removal of wet debris was precisely what our geologists had advised against.

Professor Hartwig Altenmüller of the University of Hamburg directs these excavations. I asked him if it was not dangerous to take this debris from the tomb; he replied that indeed it was – the walls of the tomb had been greatly weakened by a recent flood when rain had come to the Valley and, running down from the hillside above, had filled the tomb to the depth of a metre and more. One result of this, he said, was that the earth was so wet that there was none of the usual dust that so afflicts excavation in Egypt, and that, happily, they did not have to wear face masks!

But what about the tomb, I asked; for I had seen that small pieces of the wall were drying and that ceiling slabs were falling as they dried. Yes, he agreed, it was a real problem but he intended to continue the work. A purpose of the Institute of his University was to document tombs. Egyptologists had never studied the tomb of the Chancellor Bay, there were no photographs existing and a great number of interesting historical issues remained to be resolved. Here, after all, was a little-understood tomb in the middle of a valley intended for the burial of kings. As for rock cracks, he said, he did not think that they carried water in the part of the Valley in which he was working. And indeed, there is very little evidence in this area of the damage that afflicts the tombs lower down at the centre of the valley, as our six geologists had said. None the less, in a tomb close to Chancellor Bay's, new hairline cracks – the horizontal cracks typical of shrinkage and separation – have appeared in recent restoration work, and this might hint at slight new movements in the rock.

Kings' Valley 60 and the Prince's tomb

Completing this triangle of excavation in the Valley, I next went to visit the site of KV 60, one of six small tombs that run in a rough line down the eastern side of the Valley's central hill, the other face of the same hill that holds KV 5 and the tomb of Ramesses IX. These tombs, all of them uninscribed and made for queens or courtiers, had been cleared and re-opened since 1989 by an expedition from the Pacific Lutheran University led by Dr Donald Ryan.

KV 60 especially interested me. First, it had not been opened for a very long time and was known to contain two unidentified mummies. Second, though it was an early private tomb from the first period of the Valley's use as a royal cemetery, the maps showed that it was close to a much later tomb, that of a Prince Montuhirkopeshef, which held some of the great masterpieces of Egyptian art. Such conjunctions of tomb making were unusual in the Royal Valley, and it would be interesting to see how the ancient masons had managed to contrive their proximity.

I found the entrance to KV 60 lying under a new iron grill set horizontally at ground level in the pavement of the prince's tomb, at an angle between the great white walls of its exterior corridor (see pl. 18, upper). Leaning down and looking through the mesh, I could see a typically steep staircase of the early period: ten rough steps twisting down to the tomb's first doorway. Beyond, presumably, lay the single-chambered tomb that had been found by Belzoni in 1817. As with most of these early tombs, the ancient stone masons had chosen a spot in the Valley limestone which had a natural rock fault in it, which certainly helped their work of quarrying.

Around two hundred years later, in about 1125 BC, the tomb makers working on the prince's tomb above had filled the gaps of these ancient faults with stone and plaster. As I looked at these ancient cracks in the corridor of the prince's tomb, it seemed to me that they had recently moved, that they had slightly opened. This, of course, was only an impression. To put a precise date on small rock movements without any previous documentation or controls is unusually difficult. Here, however, there were some hints as to what was happening. When rain falls in the Valley it cements together the fine dust that usually lies in the cracks and corners of the Valley floor, and when it dries many undisturbed surfaces are left with a thin hard coat over them, like crisp varnish. This film was present at the side of the open corridor of the prince's tomb, and where it crossed the ancient cracks it had clearly and quite cleanly split apart. The last rainfall in the Valley had been in January 1991, when Tutankhamun's burial chamber had been flooded. I spent the remainder of the morning taking uninspiring photographs of a myriad cracks and floors and plain white walls (see pl. 18, lower).

If there was movement here of any kind, it was a matter of grave concern. This was just yards from some of ancient Egypt's finest surviving paintings in the prince's tomb (see pls. 16 & 17). As I photographed, Egyptian restorers working in the tomb let me in again to look at those calm walls. In those most ancient of poses, so filled with gentleness, an elegant young prince of three thousand years ago is set in amber. And how elegantly the artist celebrated his accoutrements; the exquisitely woven multi-layered linens fastened with delicate tasselled ties, that veil and reveal his slim limbs; the precisely curled wig; the shining gold necklaces; and, on offering tables laid before him, fresh green fruits and leaves from the fields, all arranged in simple harmony. No-one ever painted the reality of such things better than these artists of the royal tombs. And in this prince's tomb they were working at their full height. This then, is a truly wonderful art created by people with an acute ability to observe and to appreciate the essence of what they saw around them, and to express their vision of what lay in this world and the next. It is not an art we have today.

Back in my photographic archives, it was difficult to see if the cracks in the tomb's first corridor had moved or not. Certainly, their general outlines were old enough, for they were in the earliest photographs of the tomb. In all likelihood, indeed, the cracks were ancient – when the prince's masons had finished their work, the freshly cut rock would have desiccated and these cracks might well have appeared at just that time. Most of the old photographs were not sufficiently detailed to show if they had moved again or not. When I returned to the corridor though, a year later, and compared the state of the walls with my earlier photographs, I found that even in that short period of time there had been small movements in the cracks. In two of them, fragments of plaster and limestone had fallen from the wall; in another, a large fault that runs across the corridor floor had freshly opened, in some places as much as 4 mm [$\frac{3}{16}$ in]. These movements showed that the open corridor of the prince's tomb was gently tipping down away from the painted corridor of the tomb, towards the newly opened tomb, a situation that could arise if that tomb was drying and shrinking on its re-exposure to the desert air.

Some months later, I met Dr Ryan and asked him about these fresh rock movements appearing in the Valley's tombs. 'If that's indeed the case,' he said, 'then it's a matter for great concern.' Then, he pointed out to me that there were 'a number of variables that might contribute to damage in the Valley of the Kings,' and that it was 'very difficult to ascertain exactly which activity, whether it's natural or the results of excavation, that might be responsible for a given crack or widening of cracks. None the less,' he continued, 'if there are cracks that are indeed appearing at a time, or in the aftermath of recent excavation, it's something that archaeologists like myself working in the Valley of the Kings should take very seriously, and see what we could do if, indeed, there's a possibility that we are responsible.'

We talked a lot about the relationship of archaeology to conservation. I said that it seemed to me that the new excavations in the Valley were driven purely by the requirements of egypto-logical research; Dr Ryan considered that this might now change: 'Maybe our needs for archaeological research can be addressed while we are carrying out conservation in the Valley of the Kings, and maybe the new priority, indeed, should be conservation first.' One hopes his wishes will come true.

A FUGITIVE AND SACRED LANDSCAPE

In 1991 however, during that first trip, such dreams of conserva-tion – as yet unrealized – were still unspoken. The usual archaeo-logical priorities however, were very much in evidence. Looking down at the golden Valley in the evening's raking light, looking down from the top of the ridge that separates the Valley of the Kings from the great green plain of Thebes, I was astonished at the changes which had occurred within that sacred landscape in just five years. The low round hill at the Valley's centre seemed to be surrounded by a froth of fresh white chippings. Comparing this with old photographs, I realized what had happened – old heaps of excavation debris had been turned over and enlarged and some-times too, new ones had been piled up beside them (see pl. 21, lower). Fragments of ancient bone, wood and sand still cemented into blocks by ancient floods, lay all around them. Excavations had modified the landscape in other ways as well. New walls had been built around some of the re-cleared tombs whose doorways, though now barred and locked, were open wide and sitting in the sun, some of them with excavation dumps above them.

At a rough estimate, in just five years, there had been a 15 per cent increase in the area of exposed tomb walls in the Valley of the Kings. Yet still, no-one had ever surveyed the rocks and rock faults of this Valley with its little tombs; no-one knew the extent to which they were geologically connected with the other side of the

hill which held the tomb of KV 5 and the other tombs caught
within that moving rock-fault system. Nor had anyone attempted
to control the rate of desiccation from these newly opened tombs
which, after excavation, would certainly be accelerating; this then,
seemed like digging in the dark.

Other hazards had been unwittingly introduced as well. In
changing the Valley's topography the archaeologists had modified the ancient drainage patterns. When the next floods come
through the Valley, some of these new walls and tips will turn
and block the water, sending it directly into the recently uncovered tombs. There are other dangers here, as well. Usually, these
flood waters wash down from the desert plateau on the heights
above. In ancient times, the Valley had served as an efficient
drain, so that the flood waters passed quickly by most of the
tombs' doorways without causing them damage. Clearly, the
speed of the water's passage is critical; if it was slowed, the
chances of it soaking into rock faults would be greatly increased.
Inadvertently, these new walls and tips form a series of dams
that, when the flood comes, will block its progress for a while,
allowing it slowly to build and overflow, then crash dangerously
down through areas of the Valley which, in the past, it had tra-
versed quite easily. And as these dams fill up and overflow one
by one, the slow progress of the water will ensure that it fills
some of these newly excavated tombs, sending the flood water
further and further into the Valley rock.

The major changes in the Valley landscape, though, were not
the work of a single expedition. Over the past twenty years, most
of the pathways in the Valley of the Kings have had to be
widened and raised to accommodate the millions of tourists that
visit the tombs each and every year. When the floods come, the
walled edges on these new paths will serve as small canals. Just
as they now guide tourists down them, so will these pathways
guide the flood waters – straight into the tombs standing like fish
with their mouths open, their doors wide and more vulnerable
than ever. Tutankhamun's tomb, and many others too around
the centre of the Valley, tombs that have never before seen flash
floods inside them, will be quickly filled. Unlike Belzoni, Burton,

and Howard Carter working in the tomb of Tutankhamun in the 1920s, none of the Valley's new archaeologists have done anything to protect the tombs from flooding.

People have short memories, and flash floods have now missed the Valley of the Kings for seventy years. Here they see desert; no grass, no clouds, no signs of rain and it is difficult to imagine that the floods could ever come. But every year in Egypt, similar desert valleys are flooded; it is only a question of time before the Royal Valley is struck again.

Meanwhile, the ancient sacred landscape is fast being destroyed. The old pathways, those same paths that pharaoh's workmen made and used, are crushed under the weight of tourists' boots or buried by excavators' tips. And new pathways, worn by excavators and tourists alike, now cut through the ancient landscape. This, then, is the destruction of an unique ancient environment. Few western egyptologists seem to care about it: several indeed, are participating directly in its dissolution (see pls. 21, upper and lower).

One excavator for example, simply did not seem to know about the shale stratum in the Valley, and called the cracked mud in the tomb that he was excavating – dried sandy mud carried into the tomb by ancient flood waters – 'crazy paving'. On this expedition, productivity is measured by the weight of debris the workmen shift each day. Another, who has worked among the royal tombs for decades as pieces of the scenes that he studied lay broken on the floor, makes few public comments other than to blame tourists and the EAO for such disasters, and has done next to nothing to help the physical conditions in the tombs themselves. Another showed such lack of care, such lack of understanding of the ancient environment, that he has disfigured what was perhaps the most beautiful and loneliest section of all the Royal Valleys with ugly excavation tips. From these same tips – mostly of debris taken from inside the tombs themselves – I have recovered fragments of ancient tomb paintings, and put them into store.

After my various visits to the Valley of the Kings, my conclusions were that my warning at the Congress of Egyptology in 1991 had been timely, but not strong enough. The situation on the ground was worse than I had imagined: while the Valley excavators have their needs for scientific research and discovery, the Valley itself and its tombs have their needs too. They need protection.

How could all this have happened? Clearly, the egyptologists who work in the Valley of the Kings are neither villains nor dynamiters. They are members of a respectable academic profession, the limits of whose interest and involvement with ancient Egypt have been defined by that profession. This is the key to an understanding of how they can work at sites like the Valley of the Kings while inadvertently threatening the very monuments that they have come to study. Like most things in Egypt, the situation is the product of a long and singular history. This history, however, is a part of the history of egyptology itself.

CHAPTER IV

Study and Steal
– A Short History of
Egyptology

EGYPT OBSERVED: A CLASSICAL INHERITANCE

Ancient Egypt made its appearance in the west as a real place, quite suddenly, in the early eighteenth century. Up until that time, the Land of the Pharaohs had been a magic place, lost in the mists, like Atlantis or the Kingdom of Thule. The great romantic tale is that town by town, temple by temple, Europeans rediscovered it as they sailed the Nile, reading the tales and histories of the ancient Greeks and Romans, naming the ruins beside the river from them as they floated by. To the people who lived there, of course, Christians and Moslems alike, ancient Egypt had never been lost. The Arab writers, who travelled widely in Egypt and reported what they saw at length, were reticent to describe and speculate upon the ancient ruins, an omission born, one imagines, not because they did not see the tombs and temples, but from propriety: such ancient things were idols made by pagans; living cities were suitable subjects for proper observation.

Much as guides today are often a bridge for visitors to understanding everything in Egypt from Ramesses the Great to bargains in the souk, so the Europeans who used these classical writers as their guidebooks imbibed particular attitudes from them. Though they understood and acknowledged that their own cultures were rooted in old Egypt, ancient Greek and Roman writers often rail against the ancient land like naughty children. And those who came after Alexander's conquest also wrote of Egypt as its colonizers, as the exploiters of the land and of its people. But always, the vast reproachful wreck of ancient Egypt lay all around them, with its eccentric and dangerous images. Just as the ruins of Roman marble cities later frightened the Angles and the Saxons as they hurried through them, this colossal antiquity seemed rather to intimidate the ancient visitors who tried to reduce the power of foreign things by irony and a humour that stays with us to this day: 'pyramid' is a Greek word for bread roll; 'crocodile' is similarly Greek for lizard; and an 'obelisk' is a Greek barbecue skewer.

Just as later colonists would do, these Greeks and Romans professed to find the natives rather difficult to understand, and somewhat stupid, too. These Egyptians, they tell us, worshipped animal-headed gods and revered the same scenes that they themselves had painted on the walls of their temples! And naturally, all of them were bound by custom and prejudice and quite impervious to change, especially those changes that emanated from the colonizers themselves – that is, from Greece and Rome.

It is often difficult to discern any great difference of attitude between many of these ancient writers and the more literate of the memoirs of the numerous British civil servants who, two thousand years later, spent their working lives beside the Nile – both sets of authors, after all, shared classical educations:

Juvenal, an Imperial magistrate, on the inhabitants of towns in the Egyptian Delta, *circa* 100 BC:

> How Egypt, mad with Superstition grown,
> Makes Gods of Monsters, but too well is known:
> One Sect Devotion to Nile's Serpent pays;
> Others to Ibis that on Serpents preys.
> Where Thebes, thy Hundred Gates lye unrepair'd,
> And where maim'd Memnon's Magick Harp is heard,
> Where these are Mouldring, let the sots combine
> With pious Care a Monkey to enshrine!
> Fish-Gods you'll meet with Fins and Scales o'ergrown;

Diana's Dogs ador'd in ev'ry Town,
Her Dogs have Temples but the Goddess none!
Tis Mortal Sin an Onion to devour,
Each Clove of Garlick is a sacred Pow'r.
Religious Nations sure, and best Abodes
Where ev'ry Orchard is o'er run with Gods!
To Kill is Murder, Sacrilege to Eat
A Kid or Lamb...Man's Flesh is lawful Meat!

Satire VX. trans. John Dryden, 1693

Lord Edward Cecil, Under Secretary of State in the Egyptian finance ministry, on the same subject, 1911:

We fall to discussing the effect of that weirdest of all human phenomena, panic, on the natives of the Delta, and the way in which an oriental crowd passes in a few seconds from an indifferent, good-tempered docile mass to a collection of raving maniacs with strong homicidal tendencies. The Northern Egyptian is a curious mixture of apathy if things are done for or to him, and mad excitability if he himself has to take an active and responsible part in anything that needs action.

These, then, were the attitudes imbibed by those early scholars as they drifted down the Nile absorbed by books and temples. And they are widespread still, amongst their descendants to this day.

EGYPT INVENTED: BOOK BY BOOK

Great Thebes, the religious heart of ancient Egypt and the city close to the Valley of the Kings, was revealed to modern Europe in latitude and longitude by a Lyonnais Jesuit missionary, Father Claude Sicard. Knowledge that this legendary city lay north of the city of Aswan upon the Nile had never, of course, been lost to Europe; Thebes had merely been lost from view. In learned commentaries to the classics, seventeenth-century scholars often bemoaned the fact that they could not visit King Memnon's hundred-gated city for themselves, isolated as it was by numerous large towns and villages, many of them with a reputation for dangerous capriciousness in their treatment of outsiders. Sicard first ventured into upper Egypt protected by the janissaries of the Viceroy who were engaged upon a *razzia*, collecting taxes from these stubbornly independent people.

Sicard was a learned man, and a scholar too. As he rode through Upper Egypt, he compared what he saw with what he read in the Greek and Roman authors, Diodorus, Strabo, Herodotus, and so became the first European to recognize the Valley of the Kings from the descriptions in the ancient texts, and on the river's other bank he identified Thebes and all its temples too, half buried then, in Arab villages and towns. Sicard's outing with the Viceroy's tax gatherers was the first of many missionary journeys into Upper Egypt, journeys that took him to almost every town and temple in the region. From the very first days, he was writing, measuring and drawing everything that caught his eye:

Scarcely two leagues from Bechadé, we stopped at Ashmunein. The Bey rested under the famous portal with its twelve columns which I have described and drawn...[and] asked me to explain to him the writing done in relief on the columns, under the architraves and on the frieze. I told him that if the writings were in Arabic characters, Hebrew, Roman, Coptic or Greek I would read them then explain the contents to him. I started to examine them and saw nothing but the hieroglyphics which I well knew to be there. I gave him an explanation drawing on the ancient usage of sacrifices with regard to birds, to monsters with the heads of dogs, to globes, goblets, knives etcetera...A large part of the company which surrounded me were not happy with my answer when they saw that there was no treasure to discover. I made them see how foolish their ideas of treasure were...They served up several cold chickens for the Bey's lunch.

I have seen Thebes, my Reverend Father, its remains are magnificent and more complete than is possible to imagine. In the palace of the King one can still count nearly a thousand standing columns, a single room has 112, each one five feet in diameter, measured accurately, and is 60 feet high. The smallest stone in the floor – because all is made of stone in these ancient edifices – is twenty feet long. Outside the hall there are 6 obelisks, two of porphyry, four of granite and of an infinitely delicate workmanship... the great hall drew my admiration, it dazzled and enchanted me. I will describe them all in good time.

They say that Thebes has a hundred gates. That is more than probable; in the fortress in which the palace is enclosed one can see seven or eight entire portals, so tall and exalted, so ornate, so superb, so distinctive that they can have no equal. Each of these gateways after having charmed you with itself offers you a spectacle of sphinxes...after this, don't talk to me of Rome, Versailles and Paris.

I found whole, the two colossi of which Strabo speaks, several royal sepulchres, above all that of Ozymandias that Diodorus described, and the lower chambers were rather well preserved. These sepulchres are vast palaces where one can lose oneself going from courtyard to courtyard and colonnade to colonnade. Of the three Memnoniums that Strabo mentioned, I have seen those of Thebes and Abydos. Instead of Thebes today, there is Luxor and Medinet Habu. The river is full of crocodiles, the mountain of hyenas, the plain of Arabs and the houses scorpions. But I have seen all these creatures personally, without any damage resulting.

Sicard's ambition was to write a massive gazetteer of all the towns of ancient Egypt that the ancient Greeks had written about. Unfortunately, he died of plague in Cairo when he had only reached the letter C – appropriately enough, while working on the entry *catacombe*. None the less, with his three long articles in French Jesuit missionary journals, he had invented egyptology, that strange and sometimes ill-starred connection between western scholarship and the stones and relics of a foreign land. This is a connection by which the central identity of an ancient civilization came to inhabit not the relics that remained of it, but the words that people wrote about it.

There is a story told of a German egyptologist, one of the most eminent and revered men of the profession, who went to Egypt just once in his life when he was rather old. On the first day of his visit, he was sitting quietly working in the library of an archaeological institute. Across the room, some students wondered what they could do for this great man, and finally they went to him and said: 'Herr Professor, today is Sunday, and we would like to have the honour of taking you to see, for the first time, the pyramids of Egypt.' The great man looked up from his books, put down his pen and thought for a while. 'Why should I want to go to the Pyramids,' he asked them, 'when they are already published?'

Sicard then, is held as a founding father of egyptology not because he travelled to the east, but because he wrote about it, and his words were published. Today, foreign egyptologists go to Egypt to dig and to record and publish the relics of a civilization that seems to live far more for them in scholarship than it does in the Egyptian landscape. Egyptology began with books, and that, perhaps, is why its practitioners are still generally more interested in them than in the standing monuments.

EGYPT ROBBED: THE INNOCENCE OF THIEVES

Father Claude Sicard had always known that he was not the first foreigner to see the wonders of Thebes. Apart from a variety of Arab travellers, many European merchants had visited the monuments in earlier centuries and, though they had not specifically identified the ancient city, like Sicard they had been overwhelmed by what they saw there. 'How many and wonderful things can you see all gathered together in a superb piazza like that of Venice, which is without equal in all the World!' noted an enthusiastic sixteenth-century Italian in his journal. Later visitors, though, coveted the wonderful things in that piazza, and took them home to Europe with them.

Some seventy years after Sicard's death, Napoleon invaded Egypt. In hot pursuit of some of the descendants of Sicard's travelling companions, one of his revolutionary armies overran Upper Egypt. Marching and counter marching, they terrorized every town and village in the province. What for centuries had been a rather isolated, frightening place, was opened wide. Ports on novel routes to India and the East, small towns on the Upper Nile and Red Sea, came to serve as unlikely entrepôts for the expanding British Empire, which had first come to Egypt to expel the French. Artists, adventurers and even government committees, Lord Elgin's agents among them, came to see the fabled ruins. And what these people must have seen!

Some of the finest products of the ancient world still lay scattered through the river valley at the desert's edge. Though many of the ancient tombs and temples beside the Nile had long lain among the towns and villages of Upper Egypt, the modern Egyptians, farmers, weavers, and craftsmen, had little use for ancient things. Stripped of their gold and other valuables, many of the ancient temples and most of the ancient tombs were more or less intact, preserved by the extraordinary desert climate. In the 1820s, most of the ancient tombs of the Theban necropolis lay clean and open in the golden hills behind these farming villages, many of them with their original owners still inside them. All around them, the hillsides were strewn with fragments of their ancient burials – all those small colourful objects that the ancient Egyptians so liked to bury with their dead. Though most of the jewellery had been stripped away, much of the rest, which had no practical use and small intrinsic value, lay in a state of benign neglect resulting from attitudes of local indifference towards these ancient things. This relative peace continued until European visitors and adventurers took to collecting and marketing those miraculous survivals from the distant past.

Behind its screen of cliffs, the Valley of the Kings, too, lay largely undisturbed and uninhabited. Just a dozen royal tombs were counted by its earliest western visitors, most of which had been open to the Greeks and Romans two thousand years before them, as numerous classical inscriptions in the tombs testified. The numbers used today to designate the royal tombs – the 'KV' numbers – were painted on their doorways in the 1820s. Judging by the surprising amounts of antiquities that were found in the royal tombs as late as the 1880s, there must have been considerable amounts of their original burial equipment still lying in them in those fairy-tale early days as well. For some happy reason, the collectors who, with saws and chisels were by the 1820s cutting the prettier and more amusing pictures from the private cemeteries, usually left the royal tombs alone. Perhaps the scenes there were just too large for most of them to remove and take; and too strange, perhaps, to appeal to the European market-place of the day.

Many of these collectors, who were in the employment of the European consuls, built houses in among the ancient tombs, the better to pursue their prey. Still today, at the centre of the private necropolis, stands the ruin of the house of a Greek from Lemnos, Yanni d'Athenasi, an agent of Henry Salt, the British Consul. Like others of his ilk, Yanni spent years at Thebes, digging treasures and statues from the tombs and temples, cutting up paintings and reliefs from their ancient chapels and packing them up and sending them abroad, often to Mr Sotheby's Auction Rooms. (In western Thebes memories are long. That Yanni's house once belonged to a Greek who 'took many things away' is still common knowledge.)

Many of these adventurer-antiquarians wrote memoirs, and it is amusing to read of their quarrels and struggles among the golden hills. In their books though, few of them own to taking the sculptures and paintings away from Thebes themselves – usually it is a friend or acquaintance whose cupidity is never expected and very disappointing when it manifests itself. As Yanni put it:

...see how M. Caillot [Cailliaud] repaid me for all my kindness. Not satisfied with having copied to his heart's content whatever caught his fancy [in a splendid new-found tomb to which Yanni had granted him admittance], he sent a messenger to Luxor, on the opposite bank of the river, to procure some iron tools, with which he forthwith set to work, detaching the crust of the wall into pieces which he began sending to his house...

Yanni, of course, was saving the first choice of the wall scenes in the new-found tomb for his employer, Henry Salt, the British Consul. That the Frenchman Cailliaud tricked him out of them means that today you must go to the Louvre to see the remaining fragments rather than the British Museum.

The names of these two early competitors, and a round dozen of their colleagues: consuls and their agents, travelling Lords and officers and artists and the odd adventurer – Rifauld, Bankes, Piccinini, Prudoe, Caviglia, Salt, Belmore, Drovetti, Belzoni and the rest – run through the Egyptian galleries of the European museums to this day, either written on the modern labels or sometimes even chiselled into the antiquities that they had found and sold and shipped across the Mediterranean. Their merchandise it is that forms the foundations of the great collections of London, Paris, Leyden, Berlin and Turin.

This, then, is how the European collections of tomb paintings – those assorted fragments of ancient wall paintings, trapped now in picture frames – came into being. And their public exhibition created a market that had not previously existed for such things. By the 1820s, fashionably exotic Europeans were buying similar bits of ancient Egypt for their private collections. This destructive habit, fuelled since the 1950s by the large numbers of thefts from the Theban tombs that occurred during the Second World War, is alive and well today, part of a slow, but none the less lucrative, market in antiquities which winds through the museums of Europe and the US. (These wartime thefts, however, are not the collectors' only source today. In the 1970s, a catalogue of similar things was circulating with a list of prices quoted 'delivered to your door' – this when the antiquities in the catalogue were still in their ancient places in Egypt, to be removed upon demand.)

Ritzy art-gallery-style displays of ancient art can usually turn these sad fragments into glossy-looking works of art. That the ancient scenes are usually shown as if they were paintings, in a complete vacuum, may well encourage such damage as occurred just a few years ago when, apparently on impulse, a German visitor to Thebes pulled out a penknife and cut a painted head from a tomb wall. The British Museum, after all, was already displaying another, virtually identical example – all the visitor was doing was 'rescuing' another for the world of art. Such is the continuing disembodiment of these ancient things.

One wonders, therefore, whether or not museums displaying these fragments should display notices in their galleries, telling of the fragility and rarity of the things that they display; the story of how these fragments came to be in their cases thousands of miles from home and that – remembering Cailliaud's chisels – the rest of the tomb was inevitably destroyed to achieve their removal. Reconstructions showing how the tomb chapel appeared before the attack on it would give poetic value to the desultory fragments that survive. Many curators, though, believe that the public does not read notices at all, and there is little enthusiasm for such information. But surely, amid such evidence of plunder and destruction, there should be some kind of recognition that the subjects of these exhibitions have long been under threat, and need especial care if they are to survive outside the airless environment of a museum case.

EGYPT DECIPHERED: THE IMPERATIVE OF RESEARCH

The most famous of all these early trophies is probably the irregular block of black granite dug up by the Napoleonic armies, and known as the Rosetta Stone after a town in the Nile Delta close to its find spot. This rather uninspiring icon, discovered by a French lieutenant on a work fatigue, has three scripts inscribed upon its upper face: Greek, hieroglyphic, and a late cursive form of hieroglyphic called demotic. Quite clearly, each inscription appears to say the self-same thing, a fact that was not lost on the lieutenant from the second he laid eyes upon it. Within a month of the discovery, scholars accompanying the French Army had taken prints directly from the inked stone on the order of Napoleon himself, and were circulating them around interested European linguists.

Everyone saw that the bilingual stela could provide a key to the decipherment of hieroglyphic, the mysterious picture language whose real meaning had been lost since the first centuries after Christ. Even before the invading British came and carted it triumphantly away, various tiny fragments of its texts had been translated by European scholars of different nationalities, who were publishing their findings as dialogues in a series of open printed letters, much like Sicard's articles on the discovery of ancient Thebes: *Lettre du P. Sicard au P. De Vitry, au Caire, 8 Septembre 1719.* This formal letter writing stands at the beginning of egyptological discourse: the beginning, that is, of the recasting of ancient Egypt on another continent.

On that continent itself, of course, there was a growing competition amongst nations and individuals for the wisdom and the relics of the ancient nation that now glimmered on the edge of history – a competition that has not run its course. That we, the present writers, have claimed the Rosetta Stone as the most famous of all Egyptian trophies, is probably because we ourselves are British. A great part of this stone's celebrity resides in the fact that it was taken as a war trophy by the British from the French (a circumstance which could legitimately lead to a formal request for its return to Egypt, whose national government had no part in these negotiations). A similar French history of egyptology might claim, perhaps, that the huge stone Zodiac taken from the Temple of Dendera near Thebes and now a treasure of the Louvre, is the relic that more than any other stands for the wisdom and the mystery of ancient Egypt in its new-found home. An Italian essay on the other hand might claim that same title for the extraordinary statue of Ramesses II now in Turin – *il monumento più splendido del museo,* collected by the Piedmontese diplomat, Bernardino Drovetti, at Thebes in the 1820s. Doubtless, German curators would say the same for the famous head of Nefertiti in Berlin at whose side flowers are sometimes left in homage; a magic, strangely modern face that appears as well on Egyptian postage stamps and coinage.

Just as Europeans first struggled for possession of such icons, so the early history of egyptology is bound up with national rivalry. The great museums which store these treasures were established unashamedly as national plunder houses. The Palace of the Louvre, which for a brief while displayed Napoleon's European spoils as well, the Royal collections of Berlin and Turin and the British Museum were all favourite nineteenth-century promenades where the well-to-do strolled and contemplated the objects that their clever and powerful contemporaries had 'brought into the light'; brought that is, out of the same countries that were soon to receive the dubious benefits of European colonialism. The promenaders seem never to have been aware of the irony of their position. How could it be that they were enshrining and admiring the works of civilizations whose living peoples they generally regarded with contempt? Today, these great museums have become remarkable cultural relics in their own right; a vital piece of the extraordinary conundrum of nineteenth-century history.

At first, though, the new museums stood somewhat apart from the central traditions of western scholarship, which viewed their emerging collections as rather a grocer's vision of the past. Traditional historians held erudition, the study of texts, to be the centrality of wisdom. Memorials like Mausolus's tomb, as Francis Bacon said, might well be valid things to study in themselves, but they were of lesser importance than texts. And mere antiquities, those 'defaced remnants of history which have casually escaped the ship wreck of time' he considered as altogether lesser things – sentiments generally reinforced in the minds of egyptologists when it became apparent that the rather vulgar treasure trove of Tutankhamun's tomb had produced virtually no written historical texts at all.

Always then, the scholars took texts as their key. The ancient Egypt that this would unlock for them, of course, was literary and bound in history of a western kind, one in which the real relics of the ancient nation could only stand as footnotes and as illustrations.

Until the decipherment of hieroglyphs, some twenty years after Bouchard's discovery of the Rosetta Stone – which despite the fuss, did not prove to be the open sesame of the decipherment – all that could be said about the ancient inhabitants of Egypt was to be found in the writings of the Greeks and Romans. Then in 1822, in a printed letter to another scholar – *Lettre à Mons. Dacier rélative à l'Alphabet des Hiéroglyphes Phonétique* – the Frenchman Jean François Champollion sufficiently elucidated the structure of the ancient language to convince other scholars of the soundness of his method. Suddenly, the substance of three thousand years of ancient records was unveiled. Supported by the well-known stories of Egyptian history from the Greek and Roman writers, a basic structure of ancient Egyptian history immediately emerged which, despite many scholarly fluffs and flurries, has seen little radical modification.

The decipherment of hieroglyphs not only had a profound effect upon European history books, but also on the standing monuments in Egypt. It influenced what the consular agents cut up and put into their packing cases for dispatch to Europe. The theatrical grandeur of the early European collections had been made by hieroglyphic illiterates with a good eye. Now though, after the decipherment, they no longer carried off in magpie fashion a fine arm of granite or a smiling head. After the decipherment, all the scholars whose newfound business was the history of this ancient nation, and all the professors and the keepers of the collections, wanted relics that were keystones of their brand new scholarship. They wanted cursive hieroglyphics, on paint and plaster and always and especially, upon papyrus. They wanted formal hieroglyphics on stone and in paint, especially those enclosed in those oval rings that, in recollection of their little bags of ordnance, the French Army had called *cartouches*, and which denoted that the signs inside spelled out a royal name.

On the walls of a sand-filled temple built by Ramesses II at Abydos in Upper Egypt, rows of these cartouches carved upon a wall had long been recognized as a list of kings all written out in the order that they had reigned. By modern standards, ancient Egypt had cared very little for memorials of its deeds or history. This list, then, was a rare historical document, just the sort of thing that could be studied or, at any rate, could be set up in a museum as a memorial of study, like the bilingual trophy from Rosetta.

The Abydos King list, as it came to be called, was first noticed in 1818 by William Bankes, a well-known English traveller, collector and enthusiast. A little while later, a drawing of it was sent to Champollion, who used the text as a major element of the first hieroglyphic-based outline of Egyptian history which he published in the same year, 1822, as his letter to M. Dacier. The broken temple wall had become famous now in the halls of academe. After a few unsuccessful attempts, the hefty text, now badly damaged, was finally cut out from the temple by the French Consul in Egypt, who sent it to Paris where, in a saleroom in 1837, the blocks were purchased by the British Museum for £500. They hang now, from a wall of the ground-floor sculpture gallery, just across from the Rosetta Stone, with an accompanying label telling of their significance to scholarship and of the list of ancient kings.

It was not just ancient texts however that, with the decipherment, had suddenly become good things to own. All those anonymous faces that had stared blankly down from the walls of their tombs and temples as the collectors had rummaged about beneath them, now had names, and some of them had even begun to assume the personalities of European monarchs. Seen in this light, the tombs and temples were long galleries of ancient history, filled with royal portraits. Now the egyptologists who had worked on the decipherment themselves went to Egypt and began that long tradition of removing royal portraits from the ancient monuments for the European state museums. It seems that in one of the royal tombs of the Valley of the Kings – that of Amenhotep III – Champollion himself had some of the painted royal heads cut off the wall, leaving blank white squares in the decoration of the tomb. For many years these little portraits hung like so many postage stamps, in the Bibliothèque Nationale in Paris. Recently, cleaned and framed afresh, they were a minor sensation at an exhibition of the art of the reign of that king, an 'unknown treasure' brought again into the light.

Though these holes that were starting to appear all over the monuments of Egypt might, to the casual eye, have seemed to be somewhat random and capricious, the locations of destruction were precisely governed by the emerging science; the visual footnotes of a growing academic library. When late at night, these learned men, these scholarly monks of nineteenth-century academia, put down their pens and wiped their eyes and looked around them at the little trophies in their study, they often thought – or so they wrote, at any rate – that though this art of Egypt might not hold within it the greatness of a Greece or Rome, there was still something in these things. A trace perhaps, of that nobility that now so clearly rested in the armies and the industries, in the universities and schools, of nineteenth-century Europe.

EGYPT REVEALED: A THEBAN *AIDA*

As well as hunting down fresh historical material, the new scholars also wanted collections of smaller ancient Egyptian antiquities to join the grand sculptures and paintings gathered in earlier years. In the decades following the decipherment, barge loads of antiquities, more than ever before, were sent down the Nile to Alexandria for shipment to Europe. Naturally, the scholars used the same excavators that, earlier, had worked in the picture and sculpture gathering business, as Champollion reported in a letter to his brother, Jacques Joseph, written from his camp in the tomb of Ramesses IV, in the Valley of the Kings, on 25 March 1829.

...I must tell you that I have begun excavations at Karnak and Qurna. I am already the proud possessor of 18 mummies of all sorts and types...the bronzes which come from my excavations at Karnak, taken from the houses of old Thebes, at a depth of fifteen or twenty feet below the surface, are in a state of complete oxidation...I have put old Timsah (the crocodile), M. Drovetti's [the French Consul] old *reis* in charge of my dig on the East bank.

Time flies...Thebes, [is] the only place where you are sure of finding something really important. If I bring back something good, it will be pure chance on the one hand, and on the other pure generosity on my part...It's obvious that I can't dream of bringing back what's really lacking at the Musée Royal, large pieces, because just the cost of their transport to Alexandria would eat up my money...my means are not sufficient. It would be good if I had the funds that I asked for....

At this same time, the beginnings of archaeological conservation were stirring. Egypt was then governed by an Albanian Viceroy, Mohammed Ali Pasha, who nominally ruled the country on behalf of the Turkish Sultans. The Viceroy was not particularly interested in the departing antiquities and readily granted permission for their export precisely because the foreigners set such store by them. And by that time, foreigners were beginning to take an ever increasing hand in the affairs of the Egyptian state, and the Viceroy was relying more and more on European cash and expertise.

Even Champollion had complained about the destruction of the Egyptian monuments by Europeans. In a petition on the subject to the Viceroy, he noted that some fourteen temples had been recently demolished, 'and once they have gone, they will never return'.

Plea sent to the Viceroy for the Conservation of the Monuments of Egypt:

Among the Europeans who annually visit Egypt there are a very great number who are not led by any commercial interest and have no other desire but to discover for themselves and contemplate the monuments of ancient Egypt. Monuments that are spread along the two banks of the Nile and which today one can admire and study in complete security, thanks to the wise measures undertaken by your Highness' government.

The prolonged sojourns that these travellers must make in the different provinces of Egypt and Nubia, at the same time profit science which is enriched by their observations and the country itself, because of the personal funds they expend whether they be spent on their work, on satisfying their curiosity, or even in the acquisition of various products of ancient artistry.

It is thus in the greatest interest of Egypt herself that Your Highness' government should watch over the conservation of the ancient buildings and monuments; which are the object and the principal goal of the journeys undertaken by a great crowd of Europeans who belong to the most distinguished classes of society.

They join with the scholars of Europe in deploring bitterly the entire destruction of many ancient monuments that in the last few years have been devastated so utterly that not the least trace of them remains. We know very well that these barbarous depredations have been carried out against the clear views and well known intentions of your Highness, by agents incapable of appreciating the damage that, without knowing it, they are causing the country. Their loss has awakened in all the educated classes a concern and well-justified solicitude for the future of the monuments that are still standing.

Here is a list naming those that have been recently destroyed.

[List of temples follows]...a total loss of thirteen or fourteen ancient monuments among which three were of outstanding interest to travellers and scholars.

It is then urgent and of the utmost importance that Your Highness's conservationist views are known to your agents so that they follow them exactly. All Europe recognizes the active measures which Your Highness wishes to take to assure the conservation of the temples, palaces, tombs and all sorts of monuments which still attest to the power and magnificence of ancient Egypt and at the same time are the finest ornaments of modern Egypt.

With this desirable end in view Your Highness could order:

1. That one must not take under any pretext any stone or brick be it ornamented with sculpture or not, from the buildings and ancient monuments still standing in the following sites, whether they be in Egypt or Nubia. [List follows]

2. The ancient monuments cut into the mountains are as important to conserve as those built with the stone from the same hillsides. It is urgent to

order that in future no one must disturb these tombs in which the peasants destroy the sculptures and paintings either by stabling their animals there, or by taking pieces of the wall decorations to sell to visitors, thus disfiguring entire chambers.

[List follows; including the Valley of the Kings]

It is in these types of monuments that daily, the greatest devastations take place. They are done by the peasants whether for their own benefit or above all, for that of the antiquities merchants who pay them. I would even say that these edifices have been destroyed by European speculators in the hope of discovering some curiosities in the foundations. But the painted and sculpted grottoes which are found each day at Sakkara, El Arabah and Qurna and are destroyed nearly as soon as they are found, are ruined through the ignorance and avidity of the diggers and their employees.

It is high time that an end was put to these barbarities which at the same time deprive science of highly interesting monuments and disappoint travellers who, after tedious and tiring journeys, are left to regret the loss of so many sculptures and curious paintings.

To sum up, naturally it is not in the interests of science that excavations should cease, since science acquires daily by this work new facts and unhoped for enlightenment, but the diggers should be subject to rules that will guarantee the safety of those tombs discovered today; and in the future these tombs will be well protected against the assaults of ignorance and blind cupidity.

In the next years, this and similar appeals for the Viceroy to control the depredation of the monuments were met by a feigned puzzlement. On one occasion, he simply replied to the petitioner, 'How can I do so, and why should you ask me, since Europeans themselves are their chief enemies?'

Champollion, known as the father of egyptology, in his appeal formulated the precise outlines of the position regarding the standing monuments of Egypt that is held by most egyptologists to this day. Broadly, it is this: that as the monuments are glorious things their destruction is to be deplored; that, primarily, they are being damaged by the ignorance of peasants, collectors and visitors, and by excavations. But excavations should not be stopped, however, 'since science acquires daily by this work new facts and unhoped for enlightenment'.

As he presented his petition, Champollion, of course, had already packed his own large collections – including a considerable prize from the Valley of the Kings – in his baggage, important pieces that, after large amounts of effort and much anxiety, he succeeded in transporting to France:

Toulon. December 1829 [Champollion to his brother]...*Important business:* The sarcophagus, the large bas relief and all the cases containing stelæ, mummies and other objects destined for the Louvre are aboard the *Astrolabe*.

Champollion's deeply felt plea to the Viceroy is but one half of a highly ambiguous attitude towards the remains of ancient Egypt. It is as if, having spent his life in studying them, in some ways Champollion thought of himself as the moral owner of the monuments, with the right to dispose of them how he saw fit. And this is made very clear in passages from the letter to his brother written from the Valley of the Kings on 25 March 1829:

I come back again to the idea that if the government wants an obelisk in Paris, it would be to the national honour to have one of those in the Luxor temple (the one on the right going in). It's a monolith of the greatest beauty and seventy feet high, it's inscribed for Sesostris, of exquisite workmanship and in an astonishing state of conservation. Insist on it. Find a minister who wants to immortalize his name by decorating Paris with such a marvel: 300,000 francs would cover it. Think about it seriously. If one wanted to undertake it, one would only have to send an architect or an engineer, *practical type* (but *not* a *scholar!*). Fill his pockets with silver and the obelisk will walk.

Here then, is today's situation in embryo. Scholars wish to stop others from damaging antiquities or taking them away while they themselves continue to excavate but not to conserve, and even – if scholarship deems it of 'importance' – to buy antiquities taken out of Egypt, on the world market. Such attitudes put most foreign egyptologists in an ambiguous position in relation to the monuments. Today, Champollion's 'unhoped for enlightenment' is the currency of their profession, a step up the ladder. If historical information is to be found upon a stolen antiquity, or if it is deemed that a 'monument is best preserved away from Egypt' – a common-enough sentiment, inside the profession – then that 'unhoped for enlightenment' quickly takes precedent over ordinary morality. So excavations operating on a shoe string may choose to conduct work that they do not have the financial resources to conserve – as, for example, is happening now, in the Valley of the Kings. 'If I had to conserve everything I'd excavated,' a British archaeologist once exclaimed to me, 'I'd have to stop digging.' The root of the indignation implicit in this statement is that Champollion's 'unhoped for enlightenment' is taken as the single, proper, over-riding consideration.

Such were the tremendous depredations among the monuments in the decades after Champollion's Egyptian trip, however, that even among the consular communities in Egypt the feeling grew that the hunt should be controlled. In 1858, prompted by Ferdinand de Lesseps, an advisor to the Viceroy and the creator of the Suez Canal – and, as an ex-French consul in Cairo, someone who was well aware of the extent of the trade – another Frenchman, Auguste Mariette, was appointed as the first Director of the Egyptian Monuments.

Mariette, who had himself been sent to Egypt by the Louvre to collect more ancient texts, stayed to work in Egypt until his death in 1881. From his first year in the country, he had seen the extent of the ruin taking place among the monuments. Again, with de Lesseps's support, the Viceroy was encouraged to establish a monopoly of excavation and the taking of antiquities, and to found a museum for the legitimate collections of the state. Once the trade in antiquity was put outside the law, the public trading of the consuls ceased immediately.

Mariette then turned his attentions to the monuments themselves, most of which, though pocked with excavation holes, were still half-buried in the desert sands and modern cities. Over the next twenty-five years, at thirty-five sites, from Aswan to the Mediterranean Sea, working with thousands upon thousands of men in forced-labour gangs – the infamous *corvées* – Mariette cleared out most of Egypt's biggest temples. (Unfortunately, the most pressing problem that these monuments face today is one unwittingly bequeathed them by these great archaeological clearances; after two thousand years and more of burial and one

hundred and fifty of exposure, the dry desert winds and the eroding modern atmosphere are taking a heavy toll of their stones.)

The immediate effect of Mariette's work, however, and this cannot
be overestimated, was to change the world's perception of the ancient
temples. Once these major ruins of Egypt had been fully revealed, it
would no longer be possible to indulge in such innocent mutilations
as the removal of the Luxor obelisk or cutting sections of the Royal
Tombs away. Such things were now seen to be parts of large and
splendid monuments, integral to the sites in which they stood.

There is a fund of stories about the titanic Mariette, who not
only conducted the first large archaeological excavations in the
Middle East and established the first national museum in that
region as well, but also published a wide variety of books and
found time enough to collaborate upon the libretto of *Aida*, which
was commissioned as part of the celebrations for the opening of de
Lesseps's canal. On one occasion, when the greatest treasures from
his excavations were sent to Paris for an exhibition, Eugenie, the
Queen of France, hinted to the ruler of Egypt – in 1867 at the time
of the exhibition, this was Mohammed Ali's grandson, the Khedive
Ismail – that she would be pleased to keep the sculptures for herself which, by the rules of courtly etiquette, meant that they were
as good as hers. Swiftly interceding though, Mariette told the
Queen that she could not possibly keep the sculptures as they
belonged to Egypt. And so they remain in Cairo to this day, in the
museum that is the successor of the one founded by Mariette.

The Frenchman's passionate conviction was that ancient Egypt
should remain in its own land. It was, he said, our duty to pass
antiquity on to future generations. In the introduction to his
guidebook to the monuments of Egypt, issued in 1869 for visitors
attending the opening of the great canal, he bluntly states that
'...all excavations are interdicted in Egypt and no permissive *firman*
has ever been given...We have no advice to give to those travellers
who wish to purchase antiquities...They will find more than one
excellent factory in Luxor'. (A fact that Mariette himself used to
great advantage. To this day, some of his golden gifts to members
of the Pasha's family, clever reproductions of objects drawn in
ancient paintings, are still exhibited as genuine antiquities.)

Mariette even tried to discourage tourists from writing their names on the monuments, a fashion that began in the modern age with the armies of Napoleon, who even brought a professional sculptor along with them to glorify their names.

We earnestly beg again and again all travellers in Upper Egypt to abstain from the childish practice of writing their names upon the monuments... Seti's beautiful tomb...is entirely disfigured...[it] has actually suffered more damage by the hands of tourists in the last ten years than it has during the previous six thousand...

Mariette died while his excavations yet continued. Today, he lies in the gardens of the great museum, in a Franco-Egyptian sarcophagus surrounded by the sculpted busts of other famous egyptologists, all placed in a semi-circular display, just like the marble school of Greek philosophers that he found in his first weeks in Egypt in his excavations beside the pyramids of Sakkara.

EGYPT FORECLOSED: BUDGE OF THE BRITISH MUSEUM

Keen to modernize and encouraged always to borrow funds and expertise from Europe, by the 1870s, at the end of a long cotton boom, Egypt's spendthrift rulers could no longer pay their bills. Tormented by drought and taxed to starvation, there were many riots and an indigenous nationalist movement was born. In 1882 the British Navy shelled Alexandria, and though a rebellious Egyptian army fought against them, a British army marched on Cairo and took over the running of the country.

From the start, the British were determined that Egypt should be made to pay its debts and pay its way. Major reforms of every aspect of government were undertaken. Not since the times of those earlier invaders, the Ptolemies and the Romans, had the land of Egypt been subjected to such a stringent stocktaking. British colonial administration permeated every aspect of national life. As far as Mariette's Antiquities Department was concerned – the old man had died in the year before the British arrived – the invasion meant reorganization, higher salaries, foreign employees as heads of departments, a careful look at ticket receipts and, concomitant to this, a long-overdue assessment of the state of the monuments, which was very parlous.

Unfortunately, this newfound solicitude for monuments did not extend to Egypt's ancient cities. These vast mounds, or those at least that Mariette had left intact, were suddenly seen in quite a different light. For many centuries, Egyptian farmers living by these ancient cities had used their dust for fertilizing their fields; now this modest enrichment was industrialized. Railway lines were laid to the largest ruins so that the fertilizer – mostly ancient mud brick, crushed to dust – could be transported to the fields with more efficiency. By the turn of the century, Government Agricultural Handbooks had chapters in them devoted to scientific analyses of this singular product, and pages carefully considered its potential for the increase of crop yields. But there were also disadvantages. The ancient pottery and the 'domestic rubbish' of the cities made sieving of the dust essential, a costly process for those in the fertilizer trade. Analyses by Mr W. Hughes of the Khedival Agricultural Society's Laboratories also showed that salt levels in the dust from some of the larger cities were unacceptably high. There were other clouds about to appear on the antique fertilizer horizon, too. Hughes continued: 'The day must naturally come, in fact is already approaching, when, the better qualities having become exhausted, the poorer mounds will not bear the cost of transport for the long distances that will become necessary.' Ultimately then, it was the drive for profitability that saved the remaining ancient cities. When a cheaper fertilizer was found the destructive scheme was abruptly discontinued, though not before many of the cities had perished altogether.

In 1887 an assistant Keeper of the Egyptian Collection at the British Museum, E. A. Wallis Budge, arrived in Egypt with £500 of the Governors' money with which to purchase antiquities. Budge of the British Museum was an inveterate collector with all the tenacity of his type. As upholders of Egyptian law, of course, the British administration would have nothing official to do with him or his mission; the new administration could hardly appear to be stripping Egypt of its assets, as had happened in the past. All of which served to make life a lot easier for Budge, for he could move through Egypt with the same convenience and far more freedom than he would ever find upon Great Russell Street.

Today, when reading Sir Ernest Albert Wallis Budge, Kt, MA and D. Litt. Cambridge, MA and D. Litt. Oxford, D. Lit. Durham, FSA, sometime scholar of Christ's College, Cambridge and Tyrwhitt Hebrew scholar, Keeper of the Egyptian and Assyrian Antiquities, British Museum, it is difficult to remember, as he recounts his adventures with the Papyrus of Ani, that this distinguished civil servant is actually telling us a tale about stealing a papyrus and being on the run. But this perhaps is too harsh a judgement of the man; his antics were nothing more than Imperial high jinks, times were different, and anyway all can now be happily excused by pleading the sacred cause of 'unhoped for enlightenment'. As for Budge himself, well, this was a man who, as an obituary of him said, 'understood the Oriental, and could meet the Turk half-way...'.

Nothing can better Budge's own words, in his autobiography, *By Nile and Tigris*, when it comes to the description of his quest for the acquisition of Egyptian papyri, a description which, incidentally, also reveals much about the attitudes of the day.

Before I had been in Cairo many hours I found that everybody was talking about the discoveries which had been made in Upper Egypt, and the most extraordinary stories were afloat. Rumours of the 'finds' had reached all the great cities of Europe, and there were representatives of several Continental Museums in Cairo, each doing his best, as was right, to secure the lion's share...The Egyptian officials of the Service of Antiquities behaved according to their well-known manner...M. Grébaut and his assistants went about the town with entreaties and threats to every native who was supposed to possess any information...and some members of the Government insisted that M. Grébaut should take active steps to secure some of the treasures which had been found...They placed one of Isma'il Pasha's old pleasure-steamers at his disposal, and ordered an adequate force of police to accompany him. Before he left for the South he called upon me at the Royal Hotel, and...threatened me with arrest and legal prosecution afterwards, if I attempted to deal with the natives...

Soon after my return to Luxor I set out with some natives one evening for the place on the western bank where the 'finds' of papyri had been made.

CAPTIONS TO PLATE SECTION II

Plate 8 (upper). In the early 1970s, in the tomb of King Tuthmosis IV, paintings that had been stable for three thousand years and more suddenly cracked and split apart. The crack running down through the centre of this photograph shows a vertical displacement of the painting's two sides of more than an inch.

Plate 8 (lower). The same wall was still in movement in 1975. A fragment of the necklace and wig of the Goddess Hathor, shown in this detail of the same scene as pl. 8 (*upper*), had fallen away.

Plate 9. In a nearby room in the same tomb, another part of this same crack had opened to allow water to run down the wall, washing away some of the paint. In the royal burial chamber in the darkness beyond, fresh cracks were opening in the columns. They are widening to this day. These little-known scenes, some of the finest paintings in the Valley of the Kings, are made with a swift precision and an intensity that many of the later tombs quite lack.

Plate 10. The ruin of the great white-walled room behind the royal burial chamber in the tomb of Seti I. It started to collapse in 1960, within a year of fresh archaeological excavations inside the tomb. Many fine examples of decoration from the tomb lie amongst the rubble.

Plate 11. The Burial Chamber of King Seti I, *c.* 1920. Harry Burton's black-and-white photograph shows the burial chamber with its walls relatively smooth and unfractured, its splendid ceiling largely intact and unstained by water.

Plate 12. The Burial Chamber of Seti I in 1978. Some twenty years after the excavations, as the shale floor shrinks away from the limestone vault, the walls are covered in ever-opening horizontal rock cracks. Parts of the ceiling – those appearing as white and grey gashes in the photograph – have already fallen. By this time, it was clear that the tomb, vulnerable to the slightest physical change, was on a knife edge.

Plate 13. Another 1978 photograph of the burial chamber vault, showing the tell-tale water marks from storm-water seepage, that allowed us correctly to predict which sections of the painted ceiling would be the next to fall. The splendid astronomical scenes on this ceiling are one of the master works of the Valley of the Kings.

Plate 14 (upper and lower). Before 1978 (*upper photograph*), and after 1991 (*lower photograph*), showing the disastrous effects of the 1990 collapses. Fresh-water stains and further opening cracks – already part-visible in the 1978 photographs – indicate that, in all probability, the next part of the vault to fall will be the previously undamaged sections seen in plates 11 & 12. After desert rains, water seeping down subterranean cracks and into the loosened plaster of the burial vault will soak it, and cause it to collapse.

96

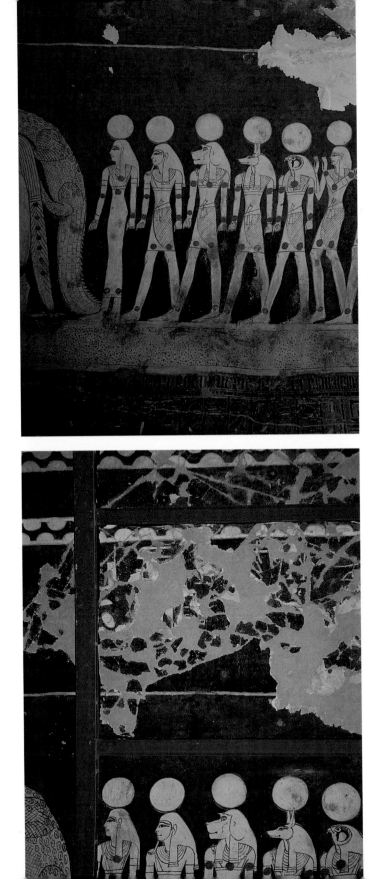

Here I found a rich store of fine and rare objects, and among them the largest roll of papyrus I had ever seen. The roll was tied round with a thick band of papyrus cord, and was in a perfect state of preservation, and the clay seal which kept together the ends of the cord was un-broken...It seemed like sacrilege to break the seal and untie the cord, but when I had copied the name on the seal, I did so, for otherwise it would have been impossible to find out the contents of the papyrus. We unrolled a few feet of the papyrus an inch or so at a time, for it was very brittle, and I was amazed at the beauty and freshness of the colours of the human figures and animals, which, in the dim light of the candles and the heated air of the tomb, seemed to be alive. A glimpse of the Judgment Scene showed...the name of the man for whom this magnificent roll had been written and painted, viz., 'Ani, the real royal scribe, the registrary of the offerings of all the Gods, overseer of the granaries of the Lords of Abydos, and scribe of the offerings of the Lords of Thebes...' In other places we found other papyri...I took possession of all these papyri, etc., and we returned to Luxor at daybreak. Having had some idea of the things which I was going to get, I had taken care to set a tinsmith to work at making cylindrical tin boxes, and when we returned from our all-night expedition I found them ready waiting for me. We then rolled each papyrus in layers of cotton, and placed it in its box...This done we all adjourned a little after sunrise to a house (since demolished) belonging to Muhammad Muhussib, which stood on the river front, and went up on the roof to enjoy the marvellous freshness of the early morning in Egypt and to drink coffee.

Whilst we were seated there discussing the events of the past night, a little son of the house, called Mursî, came up on the roof, and, going up to his father, told him that some soldiers and police had come to the house, and were then below in the courtyard...We went downstairs, and the officer in charge of the police told us that the Chief of the Police of Luxor had received orders during the night from M. Grébaut, the Director of the Service of Antiquities, to take possession of every house containing antiquities in Luxor, and to arrest their owners and myself...

Now, among the houses that were sealed and guarded was a small one that abutted on the wall of the garden of the old Luxor Hotel. This house was a source of considerable anxiety to me, for in it I had stored the tins containing the papyri, several cases of anticas, some boxes of skulls for Professor Macalister, and a fine coffin and mummy...This house had good thick mud walls, and a sort of *sardâb*, or basement, where many anticas were stored. As its end wall was built up against the garden wall of the Luxor Hotel, which was at least two feet thick, the house was regarded as one of the safest 'magazines' in Luxor. When the Luxor dealers, and other men who had possessions in the house saw it sealed up, and guards posted about it, and heard that it would be one of the first houses to be opened and its contents confiscated, they first invited the guards to drink cognac with them, and then tried to bribe them to go away for an hour: but the guards stoutly refused to drink and to leave their posts. The dealers commended the fidelity of the guards, and paid them high compliments, and then, making a virtue of necessity, went away and left them. But they did not forget that the house abutted on the garden wall, and they went and had an interview with the resident manager of the hotel, and told him of their difficulty, and of their imminent loss. The result of their conversation was that about sunset a number of sturdy gardeners and workmen appeared with their digging tools and baskets, and they dug under that part of the garden wall which was next to the house and right through into the *sardâb* of the house. They made scarcely any noise, and they cut through the soft, unbaked mud bricks without difficulty. Whilst they were digging out the mud other men brought pieces of stout *latazânah* planks, and they shored up the top and sides of their opening, which was about 2 feet square, to prevent any fall of bricks from the garden wall. As I watched the work with the manager it seemed to me that the gardeners were particularly skilled house-breakers, and that they must have had much practice.

It appears incredible, but the whole of the digging was carried out without the knowledge of the watchmen on the roof of the house and the sentries outside it. But it seemed unwise to rely overmuch on the silence of our operations, and we therefore arranged to give the police and the soldiers a meal, for they were both hungry and thirsty. M. Pagnon, the proprietor of the hotel, had a substantial supper prepared for them, i.e., half a sheep boiled, with several pounds of rice, and served up in pieces with sliced lemons and raisins on a huge brass tray. When all were squatting round the tray on the ground, a large bowl of boiling mutton fat was poured over the rice, and the hungry men fell to and scooped up the savoury mess with their hands. Whilst they were eating happily, man after man went into the *sardâb* of the house and brought out, [the antiquities] piece by piece and box by box...In this way we saved the Papyrus of Ani, and all the rest of my acquisitions from the officials of the Service of Antiquities, and all Luxor rejoiced.

When the steamer arrived from Aswân at midnight, I took with me the tin boxes containing the precious papyri...leaving the larger cases to come on to Cairo by a later boat...We arrived very early in the morning instead of very late at night, for the train was several hours late, and there were neither carriages nor donkeys there to convey passengers from the station into the town. I could not carry my personal baggage and the tin boxes of papyri...and I saw no way of getting to the town quickly, which I felt to be necessary. I got my possessions outside the station, and then sat down to wait until a carriage should arrive bringing a passenger for the morning train to Upper Egypt, which started at eight o'clock. As I sat there, practically on the roadside, two British officers out for an early morning ride passed by, and as they did so one of them hailed me in a cheery voice, and asked me why I was sitting there at that time of the morning. I recognized the voice as that of an officer of whom I had seen a great deal the year before in Aswân, and I quickly told him why I was there, and about the contents of my bags and boxes, and my wish to get into the town as soon as possible. After a short talk with his brother officer, whom I had met at General Sir Frederick Stephenson's house in Cairo, my friend dismounted and went to the police, whom I had pointed out to him, and told them to carry my bags and boxes into Cairo for me. They said that they could do no more in respect of me without further instructions, and that they were quite ready to do as he wished. Thereupon they shouldered my possessions, the officer remounted, and we all set out for the barracks at Kasr an-Nil...

In the Royal Engineers' Mess in the barracks I found Major Hepper, R.E., who had helped me so much when I was clearing out the Aswân tombs the previous winter. He listened to the story of my recent Luxor experiences with great interest, and then asked me to tell him where the papyri...were to go... I told him I had bought them for the British Museum, and that they would be paid for by the British Treasury with public money, and that I was most anxious to get them sent off to the British Museum before I started for Baghdad. In answer he said, 'I think I can help you, and I will. As you have bought these things which you say are so valuable for the British Museum, and they are to be paid for with public money, they are clearly the property of the British Government, and they must be put into a place of safety as soon as possible.' He went on to say that...he was leaving for Alexandria that afternoon...and that he would take all the tin boxes containing the papyri with him, and send them to the Principal Librarian of the British Museum when opportunity offered. He and I then opened the tin boxes, took out the papyri and repacked them in waterproof cloth, and then he had the tin boxes packed in cases which were marked and numbered in sequence with some cases of Government property which had to go with him...Before I left Cairo for Baghdad I learned that the papyri had been received at the British Museum.

As you might expect, Sir E. A. Wallis Budge is something of an embarrassment to his successors at the British Museum, one of whom claims *By Nile and Tigris* to be a semi-fiction. Even if it were a complete fiction, however, Budge's tale would still have a great deal to tell us about the mentalities of the people who assembled such vast collections. By the end of the nineteenth century egyptology, along with other ancient studies, seemed to be of such consequence, to promise such 'unhoped for enlightenment' to Europeans that it was of little import whether you robbed or stole and damaged monuments to get more knowledge, more antiquities, and more books about Egypt. Still today, the keepers and curators of these same collections would not encourage, not for a second, the airing of the question that things obtained in such ways should be returned. So the papyrus of Ani must be displayed without caveat: the role of the antiquities on exhibition in the collections remains the same as it was in Budge's day.

EGYPT SOLD: PIERPONT MORGAN MEETS THE PHARAOHS

For the most part, the European rush to remove portable portions of ancient Egypt had not been joined by the United States of America. American students and scholars of ancient Egypt there may have been, usually with fluent German or other old-world degrees, but until J. P. Morgan and his millions came on the scene, there was not a museum in the US whose Egyptian collections remotely resembled those of the European powers. Industrialists like Morgan though, and by the turn of the century there were quite a few of them, were rich enough to obtain such things, and they did. And as they did, they made a brand-new market for the past.

Morgan was undoubtably the greatest collector the world has ever known. He bought so much, so fast, that his personal whims inflated entire areas of the international art market. When he turned his attentions to Egypt, however, he operated not in a private capacity but as President of the Board of Governors of the Metropolitan Museum of New York. Morgan had taken trips down the Nile since the 1870s, and even then, as Mariette put it, 'competition to acquire antiquities increased'. After the British entered the Egyptian government, however, there were other, legal ways of obtaining antiquities from Egypt. The old decree of Mohammed Ali Pasha that had granted a monopoly of excavation to the Egyptian state and exclusive state ownership of all uncovered antiquities was superseded. Now, foreigners were allowed to excavate in Egypt once again and, at the end of their work, the things they had found were divided between the foreign institution that had made the excavation and the Egyptian Government. Several foreign governments and private societies took immediate advantage of the new rules, some of them even managing to sustain funding for their excavations by the presentation of objects found in previous work to supporting institutions – these, naturally enough, being museums. Now, excavation became big business, especially in Upper Egypt where the employment of labourers on excavations was listed in the government budgets as one of the major elements of the Upper Egyptian economy, and the monuments themselves were listed as a major resource.

Under Morgan's directorship, the Metropolitan Museum took to archaeological excavation in a big way, a progress that continued long after that strange man had breathed his last in his suite at the Grand Hotel in Rome. The splendid collection that you may see in that Museum today is largely a product of those digs; that, and the astute purchase of private collections and individual pieces on the international art market. A major conduit for some of its finest treasures was Howard Carter who, in the period before the discovery of Tutankhamun's tomb, spent many years in Luxor. Lord Carnarvon would advance him money to buy objects offered for sale on the black market in Luxor, and they would share the profit after reselling to the Metropolitan. Several archaeologists working at Thebes were grateful to Carter for tracking down and purchasing things stolen from their excavations.

Thanks to the then liberal policy of the Egyptian Government [much to the annoyance of the archaeologists, the policy of half and half was subsequently modified], the Metropolitan Museum Expedition had the opportunity of excavating at Lisht, Khârga, and Luxor, with an agreement for an equal division between the Cairo Museum and our own museum of the material resulting from the work.

So began a lecture delivered by one of the Metropolitan's most distinguished archaeologists, Herbert Winlock. Several such men spent the greater part of their active lives at Thebes digging great swathes across the ancient landscape, lifting everything in their path, keeping half of everything they found for their museum. Here then was the realization of that natural asset that the British civil servants listed in their budgets. Right at the centre of the ancient necropolis – Winlock called it a 'happy hunting ground' – the Metropolitan Museum built the finest expedition house of the time, equipped like no other. And the excavations they conducted were remarkable; Winlock's insights alone contributed more to the history of that ancient city than any other archaeologist before or since. It is hardly surprising, then, that Carter first turned to friends and colleagues at the Met when faced with the most daunting task an archaeologist has ever had: that of dismantling and conserving Tutankhamun's tomb – for never had such talent and such expertise been assembled before in Egypt in a single expedition. It is hardly surprising, too, that the staff and director of the Antiquities Organization were not a little daunted to be faced with the vision of the largest archaeological treasure the world had ever seen, excavated by the world's largest excavators and buyers and collectors of antiquities, who were, in those first days, intent on proving that Tutankhamun's tomb had been robbed in antiquity. A circumstance which, by the rules of the common excavation contract, would have entitled them to half the contents of the tomb!

As far as the fate of the monuments of Egypt were concerned, the effect of American millionaires joining the previously rather rarefied market in Egyptian antiquities, turned fragments of ancient Egypt from scholarly accessories and national icons into works of art. Morgan after all, had collected art. The Metropolitan

Museum is the Metropolitan Museum of Art. And if Mr Morgan and the Met. housed antiquities from ancient Egypt, then those too were art. Art, that is, not simply as the products of human skill and artifice, but art in the sense of things so valuable that, in their guarded air-conditioned cases, they become ethereal monuments (almost!) beyond all price. From the turn of the century, the products of ancient Egypt were increasingly appreciated for their beauty, nothing helping that process more than the discovery of the tomb of Tutankhamun, especially as Carter himself showed such obvious admiration for the quality of its contents. As black-market prices rose and rose, so once again did the incentive to plunder Egypt. By the 1950s, loose and separated limestone blocks taken from the temples of Amarna, each one exquisitely cut and of great visual beauty, were being 'accepted', as their cataloguer quaintly puts it, into private collections for considerable sums. That this relatively young art market still had a way to go, however, is seen by the fact that a superb bust of the heretic Pharaoh Akhenaten, one that stood in the Great Sun Temple at Amarna, still fetched less than $2000 at that same time. Today, of course, we know better; now the bust would fetch millions. At the time of the Tutankhamun shows of the 1970s, a gallery close to the Metropolitan Museum was displaying modest broken plaster sealings from the king's tomb, and asking considerable sums for them. Today, major museums still attempt to outbid each other and private collectors too, to purchase objects recently stolen from Egypt, and always with the same excuse: that they are 'saving' these treasures for us all. There is, it seems, an avariciousness in egyptology, to hold both knowledge and objects, to circumscribe ancient things, in print and in reality. In all this vast expenditure of energy and effort, however, the standing monuments have always come a poor second. In many ways they remain what they have been for almost two hundred years, a mine for western scholars and collectors and an amusement for their visitors.

EGYPT LOST: A CURTAIN CALL AT SAKKARA

Archaeology is a destructive act, redeemed, its practitioners insist, by proper documentation, description and publishing. As they dig into the earth, archaeologists usually dig down through time, categorizing the layers of the ages as they go, discarding what they do not want, destroying upper levels to reach the lower, keeping things that are beautiful or provide information. Knowledge, archaeologists will tell you, is more significant than a hill of sand. And who could disagree with that?

A problem here, of course, is which hill of sand you choose to excavate. As Egypt industrializes and grows, more archaeological sites than ever are threatened with damage or annihilation. In many countries with similar problems, archaeologists choose their sites by conservational priority. Safe sites, however promising, are left intact. Not so in Egypt: if they were, no-one would excavate in the Valley of the Kings or many other well-known places. Even to suggest, though, that the priorities of egyptologists should be similar to those of specialists in other areas, brings cries of protest. Enlightenment in egyptology does not often co-exist with practicality.

The Step Pyramid at Sakkara, that strange notched masterpiece of the Third Dynasty, is generally recognized as the first major stone building that humankind ever made. A mile to the north of it, along the desert edge on the great, wide ridge overlooking ancient Memphis, are the tombs of the first two dynasties of Egypt's kings; of the kings, that is, of the period before the Pyramids. Between the 1930s and the 1950s, archaeological excavations at Sakkara were concentrated on these mud-brick tombs, which held among them the modest prototypes of the Step Pyramid and hence of world architecture in stone.

These tombs, or cenotaphs perhaps, as no royal body has ever been excavated from them, were built in that amazing period when the Egyptians designed everything we think of as ancient Egyptian; from the order of their state, from writing and ways of drawing to a state religion, a bureaucracy and an iconography of men and gods alike, a system that persisted for three thousand years and more and which underlies many aspects of modern civilization. Objects made during these first two dynasties often seem to hold an incredible intensity within them; the power and concentration of one of the most creative periods humankind has ever seen. Here then, in the desert sand at Sakkara, lie the fragile remains of an intense period of human effort; the residue, you might say, of a fundamental era of the human race, and one so very little known.

The heart of this extraordinary place was excavated by a series of British-led expeditions. One by one, the royal tombs, or cenotaphs, were dug out of the sand. These expeditions made meticulous plans and photographs of these tombs, and their excavations were conducted with great care and in good order, and the books they made are clear and informative. But when they had finished working with these tombs, the archaeologists hardly took the trouble to protect them, did not bother even to re-cover them with the sand that they had dug away. Today, exposed to winds and winter rain and chemical pollution from the industry across the river, their 5,000-year-old mud-brick walls are crumbling fast. At the far end of the ridge, overlooking the line of great stone pyramids that were these tombs' successors, a heap of dust now marks the spot where what may have been the first pyramid in the world once stood: a low, smoothly plastered structure of mud brick which, when it was excavated in the 1950s, was in fine condition. In the expedition's photographs and in the careful plans they made, you can see its crisp outline and elongated pyramid with steps. Now it has blown away in the wind.

Of course, we have the expedition's plans and photographs and many books as well, and theses, too, about this fascinating tomb. But in the next century, all this data may seem as primitive as that produced in the last century by Belzoni or Mariette. And then, perhaps, other archaeologists will return to the lonely plateau of Sakkara to search for the royal tomb again, just as, today, expeditions sometimes look for the remains of monuments excavated a century ago and more. At Sakkara, scholars may come to look for this tomb, but it will be gone.

century ago and more. At Sakkara, scholars may come to look for this tomb, but it will be gone.

The west has been excavating in Egypt for two hundred years or so. We have received a myriad of antiquities to stock our museums, scholars have benefitted with their livelihoods and reputations, publishing houses and the rest of the media have gained from the public's perennial fascination with the pharaohs. Now, perhaps, it is time to give something back.

EXCURSUS: WHAT THIS HISTORY HAS DONE TO A SINGLE
ROYAL TOMB: THE SAD STORY OF SETI I

The peerless tomb of King Seti I of the XIX Egyptian dynasty was re-discovered on 16 October 1817 by the Italian adventurer, Giovanni Battista Belzoni, while he was looking for tombs in the Royal Valley on behalf of the British Consul in Egypt. Belzoni was walking across the Valley after it had been washed over by one of the flash floods that periodically afflict the Nile Valley, and noticed a depression in the ground, at the centre of which was a hole. From the pattern of sand and small rocks around it, it was clear that large quantities of water had drained into this hole, and Belzoni, who in a previous career had been an hydraulic specialist (he had arranged fountains and waterfalls on the Covent Garden stage), saw that this spelled out the presence of an underground cavity – perhaps a buried tomb. 'I caused the earth to be opened,' he later wrote, and found

the fortunate spot, which has paid me for all my researches. I may call this a fortunate day, one of the best perhaps in my life; I do not mean to say, that fortune has made me rich, for I do not consider all rich men fortunate; but she has given me that satisfaction, that extreme pleasure which wealth cannot purchase; the pleasure of discovering what has long been sought in vain, and of presenting the world with a new and perfect monument of Egyptian antiquity which can be recorded as superior to any other in point of grandeur, style and preservation, appearing as if just finished on the day we entered it...

He had found the tomb of King Seti I.

At that time, before Champollion's decipherment of hieroglyphs, Belzoni had no means of knowing the name of the owner of this pristine monument, but he could see that it was of surpassing beauty, made with care and elegance, and of an order quite different to all other known tombs in Egypt. He was especially thrilled to be the first person to walk down through the tomb's long corridors since ancient times. 'The more I saw, the more I was eager to see, such being the nature of man,' he recalled of his first journey into the tomb, 'but I was checked in my anxiety at this time, for at the end of this passage I reached a large pit, which intercepted my progress. This pit is thirty feet deep, and fourteen feet by twelve feet three inches wide.'

These pits, for they are to be found in many of the royal tombs in the Valley of the Kings, have long been a source of speculation for modern egyptologists. They are called 'wells', and seas of ink have been expended to prove that they were a vital esoteric part of the royal burial ritual. Be that as it may, in King Seti's tomb the well served the vital function of preventing flood water from penetrating its lower corridors and hence the royal burial chamber. Indeed, the same flood waters whose effects Belzoni had observed outside the tomb, had ended their journey in this deep pit. The ancient tomb makers thoroughly understood the geology and mechanics of the Royal Valley: on the western terrace above the Valley's head are still to be found the ruins of one of the world's most ancient dams which, along with an artificial cutting in the cliff, were made by the tomb makers to deflect flash floods away from another royal tomb, that of Tuthmosis III.

With the aid of a precariously situated plank, Belzoni crossed King Seti's well and walked further into the tomb. He was amazed. The walls and their scenes looked as if the ancient artists had just left their work; indeed, some of the artists had left their paints and brushes lying on the floor. It was like a flower, Belzoni said, whose petals had just opened: a 3.000-year-old flower in perfect bloom! And, at the bottom of the tomb, a wondrous specimen of portable antiquity waited patiently for the Consul's most enterprising agent: Seti's coffin of veined translucent alabaster, delicately engraved with the Book of Gates; the sacred book that told the dead king the secrets of gaining entry to the Underworld.

Shortly after the discovery, Belzoni took the beautiful alabaster coffin from the tomb, aiding its passage by filling up the inconvenient well, the water trap, with stones and rubble. After delivering this and other treasures from the Royal Valley to Henry Salt, the Consul, Belzoni and his party split in two, each taking extended trips away from Upper Egypt. Mr Belzoni travelled in the Eastern Deserts in search of mythic cities and lost diamond mines; Mrs Belzoni went on a long peregrination to Jerusalem and Syria. They agreed to rendezvous again at Christmas time in Seti's tomb, and planned to set up camp in its entrance. But when, in December, they returned from their trips, they found to their great consternation that, with the well filled with rubble, a rainstorm of the previous week had flooded the entire tomb.

Both Giovanni and Sarah wrote accounts of their attempts to stop the continuing damage in the tomb whose rock was still heaving, expanding and cracking after the floods (pp. 47 & 53, above). From their descriptions it is clear that, somewhat belatedly, both of them had understood the nature of the Valley's rock – something with which modern, highly trained archaeologists seem to have great difficulty in coming to terms. After a clean-up operation – the tomb was slippery with mud and stones – they did indeed set up house within the tomb and then, along with their Irish servant and some artist friends, they set about making drawings and casts of its scenes for a grand exhibition that Belzoni planned to hold in London. When such casts are made, however, a process that entails covering the wall with either wax and resins or gesso to make the necessary moulds, the original surfaces are often stripped of their colour and also stained by the material of the mould. As Belzoni said, 'The greatest difficulty was to take the impression of the figure without injuring the colours of it.' That he and his successors usually failed to do so, is witnessed by the many stripped and faded areas in the tomb, which extend right down through its many rooms and corridors almost to the burial chamber.

Belzoni's reconstruction of Seti's tomb, on exhibition in Piccadilly in 1821, was the first ancient Egyptian megashow. Lit by crystal chandeliers, visited by the fashionable world, it was the hit of the season. Along with its accompanying bestselling book, it made Belzoni rich and Seti's tomb, though ruined in the process, became the first icon of ancient Egypt to enter the western consciousness.

Eight years after Belzoni's discovery of Seti's tomb, Jean François Champollion, the egyptologist, visited it and read there, for the first time in three thousand years, its owner's name: 'Men-maat-ra, Seti, beloved of the God Ptah'. All at once, he realized that this was the celebrated king which the Greeks had called Sethos and who eighteenth-century histories had happily confused with the Biblical King Sennacherib. Here then, in this lovely tomb, were a hundred portraits of him. Champollion decided to take the finest back to France. Today you may still see the saw marks and chisel gouges where his workmen cut from a corridor wall an enormous relief of the king with all his names and titles; and more marks, too, on the opposite wall where his friend and fellow-scholar, the Tuscan Ippolito Rosellini took the opposite relief. The Palazzo Bargello in Florence now displays the Tuscan's trophy; the Louvre, Champollion's.

The two scholars started a veritable tradition at the tomb. From the top of its first corridor to the last passages before the opening of the burial chamber's vault, its limestone walls are pitted with ugly gaps and gashes where odd faces and the cartouches of the king have been cut out, some broken, and some 'successfully' removed. As well as this direct vandalism, the 1817 flood had caused many rock falls in the tomb. When travellers and collectors like Champollion visited it, many fine fragments of relief could simply be picked up off the floor.

Even the great Mariette seemed blind to the indiscretions of fellow members of his profession. When, in his guidebook of 1869, he laments the destruction of King Seti's tomb, he cannot bring himself to name Champollion as its principal despoiler, and repeats the same old saws; that it is tourists, dealers and the local peasants who destroy the monuments, never egyptologists:

The visitor however, will soon perceive to what sad mutilations it has since been subjected. Rumour attributes these acts of vandalism to certain explorers of Egypt [i.e., Champollion] who must, however, be above the reach of such suspicion by virtue of the very services they have rendered to Egypt-ology. It is more correct to say that the desecration of one of the most valuable monuments in Egypt is the work of dealers in antiquities, or even of the tourists themselves.

By the 1840s tourists were already visiting Egypt in large num-bers, and Samuel Shepheard was doing a roaring trade at his famous Cairo hotel. One of his earlier guests, the writer Isabella Romer, described her trip to the Royal Valley in 1845, 'which may be likened to the Valley of the Shadow of Death', when her obliging guides had taken her on donkey-back down into the darkness of King Seti's tomb. The huge burial chamber, of course, was pitch black:

and here our guide, wisely judging that wax lights and torches we had brought with us would be insufficient to give us a general coup d'œil of the locality, set fire to a pile of dried brushwood, of which he keeps a provision in there for that purpose, and the merry blaze it threw around lighted up every corner of the chamber...

Not only was such hot and sooty illumination ruinous to the tomb but it also had an effect on Mrs Romer, too:

By the time we had explored six of the royal tombs, the fatigue incidental to such an undertaking, added to the close and suffocating atmosphere, ren-dered more oppressive by the smoke of our torches, and the dust raised by so many persons stumbling over heaps of rubbish, quite exhausted me...

The march of science soon produced a convenient answer to the problem of illumination, for visitors, at least, if not the tomb. Flares of raw magnesium which burnt bright white and could be wound like string around a reel, were commonly advised for the discrimi-nating traveller. When, in 1862, the Prince of Wales and his party visited King Seti, the entire tomb was strung about with the stuff, which, with the dense smoke it produced added to the frightened bats and rats and the confusion of so many people and the strange-ness of the wall scenes, must have conjured up a vision of hell itself.

One travelled member of the Prince's party saw the slow tragedy of the tomb, and was touched by the

melancholy thought that ours is probably the last generation to see the glory of the Egyptian sculptures as they were first revealed to the explorers of the beginning of this century. Even within the nine years which elapsed between my two visits, the smoke of the travellers' torches and the disfigurement by travellers' names, and the injury by travellers' spoilations, have rendered 'the fine gold dim' in many of the paintings and inscriptions: in another fifty years it is probable that many of them will be undecypherable.

By this time, though, the tomb had long been written off as a pristine work of art – a fact that somehow transmuted its further plundering into a work of scholarly salvation. The British Museum was one of the beneficiaries of this 'salvage process' and now possesses large fragments of wall relief; some broken columns are also in Berlin; other pieces are in various museums from Brooklyn to Bologna.

Thomas Cook began his Egyptian tours in 1871 – and most of his clients visited Belzoni's tomb on their journey up the Nile, each one carrying a sooty flare to point the way. Taking their cue from the earliest visitors to the tomb, some of these tourists wrote their names in soot and pencil on the walls and ceilings among the decorations of the tomb. And many of them left dirt and grease behind them as they touched the fine relief. The British occupation of 1882 served greatly to increase tourism and, in so doing, vandalism at the monuments as well. In 1888, a group of concerned British artists and antiquarians, amongst them Edward Poynter, Frederick Leighton, Holman Hunt and G. F. Watts, convened a Committee for the Preservation of the Monuments of Ancient Egypt. The minutes of their first meeting describe King Seti's tomb as half-ruined. They sent money for an iron door to be fitted to it and also, funds for conservation work in other tombs in the Valley of the Kings. Inside a decade the Committee had become a Society, with the Prince of Wales promised as its patron and senior members of the government working to promote its aims in Egypt. Despite its generous allocations of funds for a variety of projects, however, the British administrators of Egypt did not accede to many of the Society's requests, and it was soon superseded by another organization, whose purposes were not conservation but excavation. To this day, the successor of this second fund, The

Egypt Exploration Society, remains the principal British body concerned with the monuments of Egypt and it continues to flourish and to raise funds for its surveys and its excavations as it has done for a century and more.

On 11 February 1901, part of the burial chamber of Seti's tomb collapsed, and some of the slabs that fell were large enough to kill its visitors. Howard Carter, the then rather young man who later in his life would uncover the tomb of Tutankhamun, was working at the time as an Inspector of the Antiquities Service. He swiftly buttressed the precarious remaining roof with beams, and made an examination of the rest of the tomb, an undertaking which convinced him that urgent measures were necessary to protect Seti's tomb and others in the Royal Valley. To prevent further damage from the soot of the tourists' flares, Carter obtained sufficient funds from the Antiquities Department to install electric lighting in six royal tombs, including that of Seti (a measure which, though it brought relief for most tombs, spelled disaster for the vast tomb of Ramesses X, where the generator was installed; that tomb is now barred and bolted, its reliefs, bright and beautiful in Champollion's day, are soaked in diesel fuel and deep in whitewash; see pl. 2, upper and lower). It seems likely that, as Carter worked with the electricians in Seti's tomb, he became intrigued with the mysterious corridor that runs down off the burial chamber, and that he cleared away some of the debris which at that time was blocking its entrance. At any rate, later attacks upon him in the Egyptian press held him directly responsible for what happened next. Shortly after his work in the tomb, one of the walls that supported the vault of the burial chamber suddenly subsided, leaving gaping horizontal cracks running through the wall reliefs and a v-shaped crack high in the vault above, from which a large slab of stone and plaster, with a section of the astronomical ceiling painted on it, dislodged itself and fell onto the floor.

Whatever the cause, it is clear that the shale underlying the burial chamber (see pp. 48 ff.), had suddenly begun to shrink again. Over the next three years, Carter spent a considerable time in the burial chamber, shoring up its walls. The pillared hall before the vault, which had provided some of the fine specimens from the tomb on exhibition in Berlin, was partly rebuilt in brick and a skein of steel I-bars was erected to hold its cracking roof. Lower down in the chamber, the shale that had been partly washed away from the walls' lower sections in the flood of 1817 was cleaned out and replaced with bricks and concrete. In the final stages of his work, Carter boldly put a row of car jacks under the walls of the great vault and, aiming to support the vault again, lifted the walls back up into their original position, filling the gap he opened with bricks and concrete. He was not able, however, to achieve a perfect fit; the near ten-inch displacement of the wall and vault is visible still. In the mouth of the troublesome corridor, Carter placed a succession of massive brick arches, one after another and, finally, he blocked the entrance. When he had completed the repairs he thought the work would last another thousand years. Unfortunately, Carter did not know, just as many archaeologists today still do not seem to know, the longevity of the problem that his archaeological excursion had provoked. A decade later, the burial chamber was still moving, and other officials of the department were coping with the slow, continuing destruction.

From that period, until Sheik Ali precipitated the comedy of errors already outlined above (see pp. 26 ff.), there was little damage in the tomb; or at any rate, little damage that was reported or recorded. However, since the Sheik broke Carter's blocking and started excavations, rock falls have occurred with chilling regularity. During this same period, a round dozen books on the texts and the architecture of the failing tomb have been published; but nothing has been written with the aim of drawing attention to its problems and solving them. A peculiar notion of excavating a replica of the entire tomb in the nearby Western Valley, based perhaps on the model of the Lascaux Caves in France, not only would serve to destroy a vast portion of an unique and almost unexamined archaeological environment, but would also perpetuate the old chestnut that tourists are the tombs' worst enemies. The truth is that if no-one was ever allowed into Seti's tomb again, it would still fall down because the excavations of its archaeologists have caused the rocks in which it is cut to shrink and move, and water-bearing cracks in the rocks above it let moisture pass and soak the plaster. And though tourists have indeed defaced its walls, scratched them and covered them in soot and grease, with modern methods of visitor control the problem of such casual contact could be solved. If the architecture of the tomb was stabilized, then the decorated walls were cleaned using modern conservational techniques, the results would be a revelation, an ancient splendour born-again. Underneath the obscuring dirt, much of the tomb's original colour is undimmed.

Recent outline surveys in the tomb showed that the burial chamber is still moving and that further falls are highly likely. Many of the stress gauges placed in the tomb by the EAO showed fresh rock movements between 1992 and 1993. Fresh water stains on the centre of the burial chamber vault show that underground water is still entering the faults in the rock in which the tomb lies. After the next heavy rain, perhaps, the plaster of the fragile vault will again be soaked with water and made slippery and heavy, and portions will fall. This time, though, the previously undamaged half of the vault is threatened – that, and the white room behind the burial chamber which will certainly continue its collapse if nothing more is done to strengthen it. Plaster sealings in that room, placed there decades ago to monitor rock movements, have now loosened or cracked. And when the white room falls again, the vibration from those massive blocks of stone will resound right through the damaged rooms above, with lamentable results. The tomb lives on a knife edge now. The extensive arrangements of the EAO within the tomb, new steel arches and the restoration of many of its walls, simply cannot contain the coming damage.

Since 1990, no less than three books have been published that deal with the texts and architecture of King Seti's tomb, and egyptologists give talks and lectures on it and voice concern about its ruin. Yet none of them have done anything to ameliorate its present precarious condition. In the ruined white room, just yards away from the beautiful crumbling burial chamber, there are many large, exquisitely decorated fragments of relief from the fallen walls and ceilings of nearby rooms laying part-buried amidst the rubble of the broken chamber. They do not appear to have been numbered for scholarly research; certainly, they are completely unprotected; one wonders if they have even been photographed.

Presently, King Seti's tomb is closed to tourists and is a danger-ous place in which to linger, yet it is still haunted by a poignant beauty. Western scholars who study in it, do nothing to assist the tomb's survival and refuse even to acknowledge the lesson of its history. Soon, perhaps, the fate of Seti's tomb may be shared by other decorated tombs within the Royal Valley. Like Sarah and Giovanni Belzoni though, the modern archaeologists will be long gone by the time that the big rock falls occur. By then, the full memorial of their labours will be some ruined tombs and broken works of art in Egypt, fine books and archaeological reports, and a few new chairs of archaeology perhaps, in far away and distant lands.

CHAPTER V

Greening Egyptology

PHILAE DROWNING

There was a time, not long ago, when the world cared about ancient Egypt. Cared about its survival, not in libraries or in dry museum cases, but in the landscapes in which it was born. A disaster, a well-publicized disaster, brought on this new awareness:

Work has begun on the great Aswan Dam. Within five years, the Middle Valley of the Nile will be turned into a vast lake. Wondrous structures, ranking upon the most magnificent on earth, are in danger of disappearing beneath the waters....

In 1960 Vittorino Veronese, UNESCO's Director General, launched an international appeal. The ancient land of Nubia beside the Nile, behind this great dam, was going to be drowned. The towns and villages, temples and tombs and the mostly unexplored residue of ten thousand years of history, lying in the preserving sand, were going to disappear under the water. UNESCO appealed for funds to help move the Nubian temples and for archaeological expeditions to go south in a single international campaign to investigate this still largely mysterious province. Veronese's eloquent appeal was backed by the Egyptian Government. Employing both carrot and stick, the EAO announced that the archaeologists who went to Nubia could take a half share of all that they found, as they had done fifty years before, while at the same time suggesting that foreign expeditions working in Egypt that did not go to Nubia would no longer be welcome at their traditional sites in Egypt. So the egyptologists went, and with world-wide publicity

116

and genuine scientific accomplishment, the first international archaeological rescue campaign in the world was accomplished. After Nubia, UNESCO realized its unique position: its ability to focus international attention on conservation issues. Within a few years, UNESCO was planning the listing of a common world heritage of 'cultural and natural monuments'. In 1972, a World Heritage convention was adopted by UNESCO and presently there are more than 130 signatory states and the list grows.

Flushed by the success of moving a dozen temples above the rising waters of the Nile, among them the two vast monuments of Abu Simbel, the conservationists' gaze next focused on the complex of temples on the beautiful Island of Philae. Following the completion of the earlier lower Nile dam in 1902, Philae Island, close to the town of Aswan, had been intermittently and increasingly submerged by lake waters. In those parts of the year that followed the Nile's annual inundation, tourists could sail in and around the half-submerged and dying temples. Now, the combination of this old Aswan Dam and the new High Dam, which stood over Philae as a novel horizon, threatened to submerge the island's temples completely and forever. Egyptologists helped raise the alarm, foreign governments were informed, and money and expertise was found. As the Nile rose around it for the last time, a temporary dam was built by foreign and Egyptian engineers, the rising waters kept out with powerful pumps. Block by block, every temple on the island was moved to higher ground on another nearby island, which had been re-sculpted to resemble Philae.

As Philae was taken down, a wealth of previously unknown data was exposed – a change in the usual priorities from history-driven archaeology to conservation-driven archaeology that not only retrieved fine temples but, in the process, found many interesting and unexpected things. But after all the enthusiasm for this work, after all the speeches and official openings, ancient Egypt somehow faded from the vision of world conservationism. Back in their usual hunting grounds again, the egyptologists stopped campaigning for threatened monuments. Indeed, by the 1970s a new direction in egyptology, and one most soundly based, led many of the better archaeologists away from digging at the most famous monuments, the tombs and temples, and on to town sites, which were little known or understood, and which had long been threatened by development. Today, though, it is not uncommon among the more enthusiastic advocates of this 'new archaeology', as it is sometimes called, to hear the opinion voiced that the great monuments of Egypt are finished and best abandoned while egyptologists search out new areas for fresh data. Somewhat similarly despairing counsels are behind some of the recent work in the Valley of the Kings: 'If the mountain is moving,' one excavator remarked to me, 'we'd better get what we can' – he had not grasped, of course, that in all likelihood it is he and his colleagues who are now its main movers.

Largely abandoned by archaeologists and conservators alike, many of Egypt's temples are dying, like beached whales. Held temporarily with scaffolding and old cement, they are collapsing under their own weight. Ground water is weakening foundations; columns and walls lean at ever-increasing angles; wet sandstone crumbles into sand. One method by which several of these decaying temples could be secured would be to dismantle them, stone by stone and rebuild them, properly braced on firm foundations as was done at Philae. The equipment and expertise exists to do the job again. Meanwhile, modern Egypt manages as best it can: the fifteen thousand people of the EAO tend a colossal past, keeping the temples clear of destructive plants and trees, supervising the building of supporting scaffolding and monitoring the level of the ground water. Continuously, the damp forces salt through the temple walls, causing it to break out over the surface like a pox, peeling layers of fine relief away like orange skin. Some of Egypt's finest sculptures are simply falling off the walls. The technology to stop this is available in the west – many western cities indeed, having special interests in this area, have developed treatments to consolidate the stone of their own nineteenth-century buildings that are attacked by pollution. With a few notable exceptions, though, the response of western egyptologists to these suffering temple stones has simply been to record in line and photographs the disappearing wall scenes and architecture and to publish their work in scholarly volumes, rather than to mobilize the resources of their home countries, which are considerable.

BLOODY TOURISTS?

Meanwhile, another flood has entered Egypt, a flood of tourists; and to entertain and accommodate them, there have been inevitable sacrifices. To stage Sound and Light performances, for example, holes have been drilled through temples and virgin archaeological sites dug out to accommodate their cables. The foundations of new hotels too, sometimes drive into the uninvestigated remains of ancient cities. Many monuments are continuously shaken by the vibrations of tour buses, while the day-long provision of air conditioning to their passengers means that the diesel engines are operating even when they are parked by the monuments; pollution levels from their exhausts sometimes attain alarming levels.

The World Bank loan of 1979 of almost $20,000,000 for the modernization of the infrastructure of tourist facilities in the city of Luxor, provided it with a new airport and hotels, improved the water supply and telecommunications and part-funded a splendid Visitors Centre at the centre of a new Corniche el Nil. Gratifyingly, the tourists have travelled to this new Luxor in their millions.

Unfortunately, however, just 3 per cent of this loan was allocated for the protection of the monuments that all these tourists had come to see, and that was funding for a project of tomb protection that was widely adjudged to be a failure. Presently, the World Bank is negotiating another loan with the Egyptian Ministry of Tourism for a project of 'environmental management'. This aims to improve tourist transportation, to ease the progress of coaches and boats right through the Nile Valley. Roads and river locks are to be widened and brand-new facilities created. Once again, though, there is no provision in the budget for monument conservation. When everything is done, these fine facilities may well deliver their visitors to piles of rubble where monuments once stood: the geese that laid the golden eggs will have collapsed and died.

The international tourist industry is the world's biggest, employing one in fifteen people on the planet and generating 6 per cent of global GNP. Inside the industry there is talk of the necessity for the 'greening' of tourism. Though eco-tourism, i.e., sustainable tourism, is presently only a small section of the overall business, it is its fastest-growing sector, and obviously it is of great importance to developing nations where less sensitive, more traditional tourism causes a variety of damage and destruction. Clearly, in its present state, Egypt's tourist industry is not 'sustainable'; the monuments, a finite yet essential commodity of the trade, are sustaining damage. This, though, could be changed; above all perhaps, a transformation is required in the type of information about Egypt and its monuments that is supplied to tourists. Then the present flood of tourists need not simply be channelled and controlled as if it were an unthinking, overflowing river, but could become a force for good, displaying caring attitudes towards the monuments.

After all, the millions who now visit ancient Egypt hardly wish to damage the things that they have come so far and at such great expense to see. Tourists are only inadvertently a facet of the conservation problem. Observe their present behaviour in an ancient tomb. Rarely do they look as if they were standing close to something fragile. Some touch the walls and lean against them without a thought; many brush up against the paintings inadvertently, some even scratch them with the buckles of their back-packs or their shoes. A handful even ignorantly inscribe their names. Few of them would behave like this if they were in the Louvre or the Metropolitan Museum of Art. 'Look at this,' I've heard people cry out in amazement, 'the paint comes off when you touch it!' That's right my friend, 3000-year-old paint stains your fingers when you touch it, like the powder on a butterfly's wing.

What can be done immediately to save the monuments from such devastating contact? It is hardly realistic to ban people from them. Like the new bypass, that would simply be moving the problem down the road. And make no mistake, this road cannot be shut: tourism is modern Egypt's biggest foreign-currency earner. The EAO spends enormous sums of money upon basic tomb protection with brand-new floors and railings and sheets of glass; such basic crowd control and careful garaging too, will stop much of the immediate damage. Sophisticated crowd control, however, the art of moving millions through entire environments, is a special modern skill devised and studied by a thousand international experts, and these specialists need now to turn their attentions to the rewarding task of ancient Egypt.

Ultimately, however, everything must depend upon the tourist being better informed. These self-same people behave impeccably at bird sanctuaries; in the archaeological sites of Egypt though, they sometimes fight to enter a tomb, then jam its corridors and halls as if it were a railway station.

Few of these visitors have any idea how easily ancient things may be destroyed, and in what small and finite numbers they exist. And why should they indeed; tour companies market tombs and temples as if they were consumer goods. However well intentioned, the great majority of visitors to Egypt will never have experienced an environment like that of an ancient tomb before, and they have little idea how to behave in it. If these same people were on safari though, and among the clicking camera shutters someone whipped out a gun and shot the elephant, they would feel acute indignation. Similarly, if they were on a bird-watching holiday and were told that they could not visit the nest of a protected bird because it was nervous and caring for its young, they would not insist and neither would they feel cheated at their loss. Yet, in places like the Valley of the Kings, when tourists are informed that they may not enter a tomb for reasons of conservation, small riots sometimes break out. 'What do you mean,' I've heard, 'I've paid four thousand quid for me and my family to come here!' and our tourist leaves hot, angry and feeling cheated. All this, because the public media has not provided the necessary information, the *mise en scène*, in which the monuments should rest inside the public consciousness.

The mass media tells you what things look like, reports opinions and reflects, often quite unconsciously, the attitudes of specialists. By itself, this can often be an enormous force for good. The great television nature series of the 1980s, for example, did more for the conservation of wildlife around the world than all earlier efforts put together. The reason why ancient Egypt is so badly and inaccurately served in the press and on the television screen is because the media has not been able to discover proper attitudes of care among the specialists to whom it goes for information.

Traditionally, ancient Egypt is a rather difficult subject for film makers. Though everyone is fascinated by the idea of it, to documentary makers, peripherally in touch with the professionals, there seems little new to say of public interest, and it is very difficult to discover any real stories. Consequently most documentaries are forced towards the same old clichés: a set of postcards for pictures and plot lines that show egyptologists keeping up with the Indiana Joneses; making fallacious 'scientific breakthroughs' in the desert, the like of which you will never hear again, solving the 'mysteries' of the pyramids and Sphinx and rummaging about among mummy wrappings.

Just as the sight of rubber-clad Norwegian workers chopping up whales on a factory ship in the North Sea in a documentary film no longer thrills us but fills us with disgust, so films about egyptologists digging for 'scientific breakthroughs' without a care in the world for conservation should now produce much the same reaction. That it does not, is because nature conservation is better understood than our need to preserve the human past. To change this requires real commitment on behalf of those who report on archaeological affairs in the media. There needs to be a change of attitude, certainly, from that typified by a senior television documentary producer who dismissed the need for conservation-conscious documentaries recently with the phrase, 'Well, of course, I made a film about conservation years ago.' The truth is, there should be no other kind of reportage about our past other than that which shows it to be precious to us: precious and fragile too. Presently this it not true, and that is why people save whales and scratch monuments.

Ultimately, the modern identity of ancient Egypt must be changed. Changed from the wacky world of Indiana Jones and Wallis Budge snatching treasures and 'unhoped for enlightenment' from the 'natives' and taking them off to civilization. Changed, so that feature films with stumbling mummies and caricatured befezzed Egyptians themselves appear to be antique. Changed, in fact, in the same way that shooting tigers has changed from being the sport of kings to being considered an ignorant and savage act. Given the present straits of ancient Egypt, the same media that so boldly and so cleverly reports the problems of natural conservation would be well advised to esteem egyptologists a little less, and question their procedures and their attitudes rather more.

ATTITUDES

Sitting in the halls of the Turin International Congress of Egyptology in 1991, one quickly gained the impression of observing an anachronism, a shadow of something that used to be. All of which would possess its own strange charm, were it not for the fact that the shell and substance of its study, the standing monuments of ancient Egypt, are in extraordinary straits and these scholars, the professionals who many would naturally consider as their guardians and international champions, do precious little to help and indeed, as in the Valley of the Kings, sometimes actually aggravate a dangerous situation. This, then, is a rather elderly and remote profession, lost in study: like archaeology, much of its work is incredibly exacting, and this sometimes creates rather obsessive attitudes in its practitioners which, by their very intensity, tend to obscure the wider view.

The attitudes of these specialists, of course, are given to the public largely unconsciously and at second hand. Museums especially have an important role in this as they are the places where people first 'experience' ancient Egypt as they 'experience' Picasso or 'Medieval Art'. In modern museums, ancient Egypt is a lot like Breakfasting at Tiffany's; in older museums, it's a rough-and-tumble trip from school. All of which imparts nothing of the real modern story of ancient Egypt – that it is disappearing fast. An environment like the mummy rooms of the British Museum, for example – the world's most visited museum space it is proudly counted – provides a quite specific atmosphere for visitors. It also serves as an introduction to British attitudes in colonial Egypt; one of Wallis Budge's trophy rooms, with case loads of dead Egyptians, with classes of children running past their coffins and adults pushing and bumping against the walls as if in training for a trip to the Valley of the Kings. Do we really have a right to view the past in such a way? Is this really how we wish to treat it? As an introduction to ancient Egypt, it strips it of its dignity, and, in so doing, helps create the attitude to standing monuments that you see in Egypt every day.

Modern museums of natural history, on the other hand, present arguments for care and conservation as an integral part of their displays. Here, of course, as at modern zoos, conservation is a vital ingredient of the subject. In consequence, modern children are more engaged by the power and dignity of elephants and whales than they are by the monuments made by their own kind.

It is significant that, of the hundred or so foreign egyptological missions working in Egypt, just one, the Getty Conservation Institute of Marina Del Rey California, has conservation as its exclusive purpose. As for the others, their names alone sometimes tell the story: the British society – The Egypt Exploration Society – explores Egypt; the US body – American Research Centre in Egypt (ARCE) – researches it. As the annual reports in their respective journals show, neither put a high priority on conserving ancient Egypt, certainly not at sites they have not themselves excavated. Dr Terry Walz, the New York Director, describes ARCE's operations so; 'The American way is to let individuals, academic institutions and foundations like the "Getty" do their own thing without direct governmental involvement.' He readily agrees that usually this hardly includes conservation, though as he pointed out to me, ARCE has initiated a special conservation fund, though when I last checked, the sum it held would not have bought five library shelves, let alone the books to put on them. Compared with some of the European national institutes in Egypt who fund major conservation projects as an integral part of their work, both British and US activity is minimal.

Unwittingly, the British and US systems also lend themselves to the exploitation of the monuments. If, for example, an individual archaeologist leaves his site half excavated or worse, unprotected and unconserved, and goes to work in another country (and this is not uncommon), there is no-one in Egypt from whom the Egyptian authorities can seek redress. As some recently excavated tombs in the Valley of the Kings may well be the cause of problems in the future, this may soon become a live issue. British and American excavators do not work under the aegis of their governments in national institutes as do most European excavators, and there is therefore no guarantee of a continuity of working or long-term conservation, even of the things they excavate.

The problem is not a new one. Even before the First World War, the great British egyptologist, Sir Alan Gardiner, wrote in a preface to a publication dealing with the private tombs of Thebes:

That Egyptologists in the past should have been permitted to dig out tombs to satisfy a mere caprice, and without giving any undertaking to protect and publish what they found, is in the highest degree deplorable. It would be easy to point to a dozen tombs that have thus been excavated, and, after a few inscriptions have been copied, abandoned to their fate without a thought...it is [also] highly undesirable that any hitherto undiscovered decorated tombs should be unearthed; we have already so large a number to cope with, that it is far better that a halt should now be called to excavation and that we should continue all our energies upon the study of what has been rescued.

A traditional response of egyptologists when faced with fast-decaying monuments has been to draw them, in extraordinary detail, and publish them in specialist literature. This is what Professor James Henry Breasted, Carter's distinguished guest in the first days of the re-opening of the tomb of Tutankhamun, called 'saving the past', though one imagines that Carter, a clever and committed conservator of ancient things, could hardly have agreed with him. For seventy years, however, since Breasted first raised money from John D. Rockefeller Jr, and still today, the University of Chicago's Epigraphic Survey has been drawing ancient Egyptian tombs and temples. For fifty years, at a cost of millions, the Survey worked in the temples of Medinet Habu on the west bank at Thebes: in more recent decades, it has concentrated its activities in the crumbling Temple of Luxor on the east bank of the river. The Survey's drawings are faithful facsimiles of the original ancient reliefs, accurate, it is said, to within hundredths of an inch. As you may imagine, such techniques are labour intensive and always extremely expensive.

The Survey's present Director, Dr Peter Dorman, acknowledges that the huge prestigious volumes that they produce may well last longer than the ailing temple in which they work. He and other members of the Survey have watched the temple's stones 'gradually disintegrating before our eyes', while they make their drawings of the reliefs cut upon them. His drawings, he feels, are a conservation measure in themselves – here we have returned to Breasted's notions of what 'saving the past' entails – an attitude with which Dr Vivian Davies, Keeper of Egyptian Antiquities at the British Museum, readily concurs (see. p. 33) while also noting that those who would protest about merely documenting monuments as they crumble are simply 'oversensitive'.

Despite such protestations, though, this really is pure fantasy: instead of saving the monuments, egyptologists are happily turning them into a library and claiming this to be an act of conservation. The truth is that, as a response to the tragic situation arising in the Egyptian monuments, no amount of drawing and measuring would answer. Drawings cannot be a substitute for the real thing. Ancient Egypt is not a library, any more than is Florence or Kyoto. To suggest that you can 'save the past' by making facsimiles of selected parts of it, is as ridiculous as saying that Monte Cassino and Coventry and Dresden are all preserved because we have film of them before their bombing or that we no longer need horses because we have *Life on Earth*, and Stubbs's drawings of their anatomy. So preposterous indeed, is this idea, that one begins seriously to question the intellectual value of a profession that, in the very areas of its expertise, does not expect to differentiate between pale copies and the real thing. The sad thing is, of course, that even though this present generation of scholars may not be able to tell the difference, the chances are that others will: and then it may be too late for everyone.

It is not that egyptologists do not care about the condition of the monuments. It is simply that they have their own version of ancient Egypt, another version, whose orderly reality is largely confined to libraries and museums. They have put their energies into studying this cloistered version of ancient Egypt, its language, its literature, its history. These peaceful and secluded studies are often ratified by a progression up the academic ladder. Coming to terms with crumbling stone and encrustations of salt eating away inscriptions in a foreign land is a situation with which, on the whole, they are reluctant to deal, even if they live and work amongst the monuments themselves. This, after all, is not a profession of engineers or geologists, but traditionally minded scholars.

None the less, these same people, who most of us would regard as the experts on these crumbling monuments, are often most reluctant to give up the role of public guardian which they have been inadvertently awarded. We often hear, therefore, of 'research programmes not completed' or of 'more study required before conservation measures can be taken' as if they were actively involved in solutions to the problems of the monuments; in reality, most of them are not. And, let's face it, very few of them have ever tried. Some indeed are hostile, others apathetic. If the professionals wish to continue in the role of public guardians of the monuments, it would be good to see rather more than 1 per cent of the papers delivered at the next International Congress of Egyptology dealing with subjects of site conservation, as was the case at the last congress. It would be good, too, if conservation was counted as a necessary requirement for university degrees in egyptology.

PRIORITIES

Certainly, archaeological granting agencies should look much harder at conservation issues, and private sponsors of small expeditions should consider whether or not their money will help or hinder the survival of the monuments. It is likely, for example, that the regulations of many nations would not permit on their own soil some of the archaeological activities they fund in Egypt, and one wonders therefore whether their infraction outside the boundaries of the home country, often with the use of public moneys, is even legal.

When faced with the realities of conservation, many foreign egyptologists plead that their under-funded profession cannot

CAPTIONS TO PLATE SECTION III

Plate 15. Workman sorting through the tip of the University of Hamburg excavations in 1992. The darker coloured sand in the foreground of the photograph is damp, having been freshly brought out into the sunlight from the depths of the nearby tomb of the Chancellor Bay.

Plates 16 and 17 (upper and lower). The tomb of Prince Montuhirkopeshef, one of the greatest gems of ancient Egyptian painting, seen here during the geological survey of the Valley conducted in 1979.

Plate 18 (upper). The same tomb doorway in 1989, after the excavations of the Pacific Lutheran University opened a small tomb, cut hundreds of years before the prince's lifetime, in the entrance of his tomb.

Plate 18 (lower). Within a year of the excavation, several of the old cracks in the entrance corridor of the prince's tomb were moving and opening – these just yards from Montuhirkopeshef's tomb decorations.

Plate 19. The two grooves in the hill in the middle ground of the photograph are part of a water-carrying rock-fault system that runs straight into the centre of the Valley of the Kings and through some of its most celebrated tombs. (Part of the doorway of the tomb of Ramesses VI, the tomb adjacent to that of Tutankhamun, is visible behind the upper fault.) One of the tombs presently under excavation (1993) in the Valley of the Kings, number KV 5, lies under this hill and is cut into this same rock-fault system. Two separate projects plan to excavate further into tombs in this same fault system. Between them, they entail the removal of more than 3000 tons of debris from the Valley, at least half of which has recently been soaked in water from a defunct sewage system. These two excavations, one planned, one in progress, are probably the largest single threat presently facing the Royal tombs.

Plate 20 (upper and lower). Two views of the entrance of the tomb of Tutankhamun's predecessor, King Ay, cleared in the early 1970s by an expedition from the University of Minnesota. After work had finished, the tomb's entrance was completely blocked with huge boulders, some of which appear to have been rolled down into the doorway, damaging the staircase. Twenty years on, the tomb's exterior presents a sorry sight, the ruined interior still awaiting full conservation.

Plates 21 (upper and lower). The ancient landscapes of the Royal Valley have suffered greatly from the archæological activities of the last ten years. These two views were taken in 1981 *(upper)* and 1992 *(lower)*. While some of these changes have been made to accommodate vastly increased tourism, parts of the Valley not visited by holiday-makers have also been changed beyond recognition. By opening more tombs, creating new pathways, building stone walls and enlarging old excavation tips, the Pacific Lutheran excavations have transformed the lateral Valley in the pictures' foregrounds.

Plate 22. The great green Osiris of the Tomb of Ramesses I, in the shadows of the restorer's scaffolding.

possibly cope with such enormous tasks as moving temples or monitoring valleys filled with tombs. Yet today, sections of this same profession competently organize international exhibitions and build multi-million-dollar libraries and accommodation (from which each day, they sally forth to study and draw the crumbling monuments). Surely this profession is capable of joining the Egyptians in the task of conservation; and if they are not or do not wish to do so, the public or the public's appointed officers should perhaps change the people whom they appoint to guard the past.

In years gone by, it sometimes seemed as if archaeologists enjoyed rights in Egypt that had hardly changed since the days of the Consuls in the last century. Recently though, many EAO officials have become increasingly concerned at the activities of some foreign missions. It has been suggested, for example, that foreign archaeological expeditions should be required to undertake conservation projects when they are issued with permits to excavate, and that all fresh sites for excavation should be selected strictly according to conservation requirements. It has also been proposed in Egypt that, given the present emergency, unless conservation is taken more seriously by foreign archaeological missions, a ten-year moratorium on excavations other than those of rescue archaeology would be appropriate. New regulations for foreign missions working in Egypt are expected to be announced by the EAO in the near future.

If such important changes of direction were to take place, conservation-driven archaeology would still unearth 'unhoped for enlightenment'. Just a few years ago, for example, Egyptian conservationists taking soil samples beside the tilting columns of the Luxor temple struck hard stone some six feet under the floor of the great open court. Archaeological investigation soon revealed the group of extraordinarily beautiful statues now displayed in a special room at the Luxor Museum. Such sculptures are a rare sight indeed, what you might call brand-new ancient statues. These fresh masterpieces from the Luxor temple, filled with dignity and human warmth, are as fine as any of the celebrated masterpieces of the period. They give us just a hint of what might be found if it was deemed desirable to dismantle Luxor temple for its conservation.

Almost every one of the Egyptian temples stands on earlier temples and many, surely, hold caches of statues similar to that of Luxor, and sometimes, doubtless, in much larger numbers. Every time you conserve a tomb or a temple you will find new things.

CO-OPERATION

With a few honourable exceptions, the various French and the German missions being the outstanding examples, foreign expeditions in Egypt usually only conserve things that they have themselves excavated or recorded, and there is minimal co-operation with the EAO departments and officials.

Not far from the crumbling Luxor temple, however, just across the river, Dr Christian Leblanc of the Centre National de la Récherche Scientifique du France is working with colleagues from the EAO in that beautiful and celebrated temple, the Ramesseum. He is a new type of foreign egyptologist, one who does not exploit the monuments in the name of his profession. Dr Leblanc works closely with the Documentation Centre of the EAO, raising money and expertise from France whenever necessary, and always in collaboration with members of the local Antiquities staff. As well as completely cleaning this major Egyptian temple for the first time since the days of Mariette – an exercise that has already produced a wealth of fresh egyptological information and some interesting works of art – the project is a pilot scheme for other conservation projects. Almost immediately, the work paid off. Temporary buttresses placed under some of the temple's cracked stone lintels supported the masonry during the recent Egyptian earthquake. Similar pieces in less-protected monuments fell and were smashed to fragments.

Standing with this mission in the temple as they worked, one could observe the excellent co-operation between French and Egyptian colleagues, architects, egyptologists and excavators alike. Such collaboration is rare on sites in Egypt and this is sad, because there is much experience to be gained on both sides and much evaluation to be done too, on the ground, at the precise point where foreigners are introducing new materials and techniques. Of the five archaeological teams working in the Valley of the Kings, for example, not one of them collaborates with their Egyptian colleagues. Neither are any of them engaged in any conservation other than that of securing the safety of the tombs in which they are actually working. At this same time the EAO officials continue the expensive task of protecting nearby tombs from the onslaught of multitudes of visitors. Certainly, there is little in the way of common effort in the Valley and virtually none of the foreign expeditions want to join this work of conservation. So the Egyptians, surely the most generous of hosts, soldier on by themselves.

Nowadays, unlike the tombs of the Valley of the Kings, no-one would seriously question the security of the vast Temple of Karnak, perhaps the largest temple in the world, set close to Luxor temple, but in a very different state of conservation. Since the turn of the century, joint French and Egyptian Government missions have successfully conserved and cared for Karnak. The emphasis has always been on conservation and reconstruction as the present splendour of the temple shows. Today, the Egyptian Government supplies egyptologists, staff, the workers and materials: the French provide additional architects, engineers, hydrologists and stone conservators. The employment of recently developed imported equipment that employs abrasion techniques of infinite subtlety is bringing life back to painted reliefs long covered by the grime and soot of the ancient town that once stood around the temple. One of the major problems of Karnak has long been ground water; for many years now the staff of the *Centre Franco-Egyptien* have made in-depth studies as to how the problem arises and much work has being done establishing new techniques for dealing with wet stone. The stones of Karnak, indeed, have suffered far more than their fair share of degradation. Presently, the *centre* has a scheme to build a chemical plant, the first in Egypt, to produce a compound that is presently available only in small expensive quantities and imported from abroad. This substance will serve to strengthen Karnak's crumbling stones. Other treatments, too, are being formulated for stone conservation and these between them, perhaps, offer some of Egypt's other ancient temples the greatest chance for their survival.

KINGS' VALLEY CODA

Every site in Egypt is unique. Today, each one of them has its own special problems. As for the Valley of the Kings, its first requirement is that some of the tombs need immediate expert attention; emergency measures, for example, to prevent the vault of King Seti's burial chamber smashing onto the floor after the next rainstorm. In the longer term a complete geological survey and the placement of monitoring equipment in the tombs is required and subtle engineering work is needed to stabilize the valley rocks. The solution to the stability of Seti I's great burial chamber might include its suspension from the natural rock above it, freeing it from the unstable support of the underlying shale. Clearly, too, the problem of water-carrying rock faults needs solution. Fortunately, there are simple and inexpensive answers to this last problem.

Certainly, archaeological clearance, a wild card in the Royal Valley in its present unstable situation, should be postponed, and, to contain the possibility of the continued desiccation of the rock, recently excavated tombs should be sealed shut again. One bonus from this halt in excavation might be that competent displaced archaeologists go north to work. Concerned archaeologists regularly implore their fellows to work in the Egyptian Delta before unavoidable development swiftly eliminates sites that they believe contain unknown chapters of Egyptian history.

One of the Valley's present tragedies is that the expeditions working there look only to their own little plots: the Valley of the Kings, of course, is a single unified environment; a single water course; a single geological entity; a single archaeological milieu. Any new feature, from a lamp post on a tourist path to an excavation tip by a newly opened tomb, may threaten damage to the landscape and its tombs – if not by changing the water levels in the rocks as excavation does, then more brutally and more directly, by acting as a funnel or a deflector during the flash floods that, one day, will visit the Valley once again. So, to answer the Valley's needs, traditional egyptology should transform itself and participate in a larger and more humane subject – the overall management of the entire site. And this perhaps might be most efficiently achieved by a collaborative effort similar to those that are presently so successful at Karnak and the Ramesseum.

Clearly, after a hundred years of heavy tourism, many of the royal tombs need elaborate conservation, their paintings require cleaning and stabilizing. Here there are already chinks of light. Complimenting decades of work in the Valley by the conservators of the EAO, the Getty Conservation Institute now plans to consolidate and clean the paintings in the Tomb of Tutankhamun and, at the same time, initiate a training programme for local students in the use of newly developed techniques in this delicate and time-consuming work.

With all of this activity, a vital requirement of those working in the Royal Valley would be a full data bank: files of all available information on the Valley, whose study will establish in far greater detail than anything we now possess the physical history of the landscape and its tombs. Up-to-date records are essential, too. We have short inaccurate memories for things like cracks and colours, and it is impossible to accurately recall how things were inside the tombs. Old photographs of the burial chamber of King Seti, for example (see pl. 11), show it almost free of the myriad cracks that now afflict it; when you study these pictures you suddenly realize what has happened to these tombs.

In the longer term, too, the Valley must be made safe from the threat of ruinous flash floods. Its floor must be kept free of obstacles so that water can move straight through it with a minimum of damage. Deep-lying tombs, like that of Tutankhamun, might be fitted with waterproof doors. A simple method of keeping flood water from the doors of many of the larger tombs would be to lower the present pathways in the Valley. These were levelled out in the 1920s, and are composed of ancient chippings mixed with the dirt of excavation. This lowering, though, could only take place after full studies of the geology of the Valley have been made and would have to be accompanied by extensive monitoring throughout the tombs.

As for the continuing flood of visitors; projected figures for Egyptian tourism predict that numbers will double within five years. As greater numbers of properly protected tombs are opened in the Royal Valley, as is presently happening, the numbers of visitors in any one of them is quickly thinned. If, however, future numbers increase beyond all reason, other drastic steps are planned. One scheme presently under discussion is that visitors should only view one tomb each day, and that by prior appointment, in the manner of booking a seat at a theatre.

The Valley of the Kings really can be helped to flourish once again. Not one of its problems is without solution. At the moment, though, the west is a part of these problems, rather than a part of their solution. And that seems to me to be entirely unacceptable.

If we do not rally to the aid of sites like the Valley of the Kings, in twenty-five years most of them will be ruined. And our children will sense this loss, as we today cannot. For when that ancient land and all its monuments have died, a part of us, a part of our humanity, will have died as well. And then they will wonder, how on earth did something like that ever happen? But then it will be too late.

Do you not know that Egypt is a copy of heaven, and the temple of the entire world? Yet there will be a time when it will be seen that it was in vain that the Egyptians cherished the gods, that all their holy reverence was to no effect. This land which was the home of worship will be stripped of its gods and left bare, and foreigners will fill this region. Then this most holy land, the abode of shrines and temples, will be filled with graves and dead men.

Appendices

APPENDIX ONE

HISTORY AND EXPERIENCE IN THE VALLEY OF THE KINGS
(1991)

Paper presented at the International Congress of Egyptology,
Turin, Italy, September 1991

1. A SERIES OF PHYSICAL SURVEYS OF THE VALLEY OF THE KINGS were conducted during 1977–9 [1], prompted by damaging new rock movements in the royal tombs that were splitting walls, detaching tomb paintings and threatening the collapse of rooms and corridors. These surveys described the basic mechanisms of the geological processes that continue to damage and destroy these great monuments, and criteria were established to monitor and control them. However, recent archaeological activity in the Valley shows very little awareness of this work. Indeed, several current and projected enterprises will actually accelerate and multiply rates of destruction in the royal tombs beyond anything yet seen. This paper, therefore, outlines relevant sections of the reports of the 1977–9 Surveys, pinpoints present dangers and outlines procedures to minimize future damage of the royal tombs by archaeologists.

2. THE GEOLOGIC ENVIRONMENT OF THE ROYAL TOMBS was determined by primeval flood waters cutting the Valley from the lowest of the four limestone terraces of the Theban Gebel. Curtis observes that many of the tombs' doorways are excavated in the 'lowest marly limestone bed' laying immediately above a 50-metre shale

stratum – 'the so-called Esna Shale that is such a distinctive fea-ture of western Thebes'. [2] The tomb makers excavated many of the tombs' burial chambers so that their floors exposed one of the thin bands of reddish shale that lie a few metres above the grey main stratum. Most of the Valley's tombs are close to these unstable strata; typically – as in the tombs of Seti I and Ramesses II – many of the burial chambers' walls and columns are cut from limestone rock units that stand upon the softer and friable shale of the floor. Here perhaps, in view of the extraordinary problems these circumstances pose us, it should be stressed that the geology of the Valley of the Kings is probably unique amongst all the major archaeological sites of Egypt.

3. THE PHYSICAL PROPERTIES OF THE VALLEY'S ROCK, both shale and limestone, were quantified in laboratory tests. [3] The shale espe-cially, is highly expansive: when it is saturated, this action is severe enough to cause disintegration. Though less dramatic, the effect of water upon the limestone was found to be similar. Fortu-nately, these tests also indicate that these ruinous processes of expansion are triggered only by contact with liquid water: high humidity levels, a common consequence of mass tourism in tombs, did not serve to increase the water content of the samples tested and thus, did not promote swelling or disintegration. However, these tests also demonstrate that the Valley's rocks desiccate and contract substantially when in contact with dry air – a fact that in the past has lead to the collapse of many tombs, sometimes decades after their archaeological clearance. The absorption and expansion properties of Valley rock are of fundamental importance for the conservation of the royal tombs and should therefore be a constant preoccupation of all who work in the Royal Valley.

Even as the tombs were quarried, the initial exposure of the liv-ing rock caused it to lose its natural humidity levels, to dry, con-tract and crack, prompting rock falls whilst the work yet continued. This process was studied in some detail in the Survey's test-bed tomb of Ramesses XI, where surfaces usually covered by plaster and paint were left exposed. The massive cracks in the doors, lintels, ceilings and pillars of this tomb may be considered as typical for other royal tombs as well; future workers should therefore expect to encounter such weaknesses under the plaster and decorations of more famous monuments. [4] This ancient desiccation was found to have produced elaborate three-dimensional crack patterns radiating outward from the tombs and forming complex secondary fracture systems between the larger rock faults of earlier geologic epochs. Curtis shows that these various rock-fault systems all serve as conduits that conduct storm water and alluvial sand from above the Valley down into the tombs. [5]

4. FLOODING IN THE ROYAL TOMBS. Until the last century, the Royal Valley functioned as a relatively efficient drain, allowing flash floods from the high desert to pass quickly through the areas of the tombs. [6] Most tombs, however, show some flood damage, and some have been destroyed by it; Ramesses II's tomb, for example, was entered on at least ten occasions by floods and debris flow before its doors were themselves buried in debris. Untypically, there have been no major floods in the Royal Valley for some seventy years. Unfortunately, this same period of time has seen major modifications to the Valley's landscape. The opening of tourist paths and a wide variety of archaeological work has raised present flood-water paths to the exact height of most of the tombs' doors. When the floods return, the Central Rest House will act as their breakwater, directing them straight into the tombs of Tutankhamun and Ramesses VI – these being but two of the celebrated monuments which, though they have not yet seen large-scale water intrusion, are today more vulnerable than ever.

5. THE 1977–9 SURVEY OF PRESENT FLOOD PATTERNS. Monaghan describes two principle types of flooding in the tombs; one, a massive abrasive flow of liquid aggregate from the surrounding hillsides studded with boulders and tomb quarriers' chippings, and a secondary, comparatively gentle flood in which light sand-carrying streams run straight down into the tombs' burial chambers. [7] The tomb makers, and, later, the Valley's early archaeologists, all saw the devastating effects of flooding within the Royal Tombs. Dams, dykes and barriers of rock and boulders show that all these people appreciated this ever-present threat. Romer notes that though living memory of these deluges has all but disappeared 'the evidence ... of the literature and the experience of the geologists

informs us that the Valley of the Kings is prone to flooding, has flooded and will certainly flood again'.

6. SUBTERRANEAN FLOODING IN THE TOMBS along rock faults (paragraph 5, above) is a frequent phenomenon. The tomb of Ramesses III, for example, has been flooded from the burial chamber outward; the lower sections of this tomb was completely filled with water and destroyed. In 1991, another rock fault conducted smaller amounts of water into Tutankhamun's burial chamber. [8] The burial chamber of Ramesses III filled with water between 1883 and 1910. Immediately, the shale of the floors in the tomb's lower sections thrust up with tremendous force, pushing the limestone walls and columns against the rock mass above, causing massive fracturing and collapse. During the next century, as these chambers slowly desiccated, shrinkage caused further extensive rock falls. At the time of the survey, blocks of the burial chamber were hanging loosely, still sensitive to the lightest vibration. Recent work in the tomb has made it safer, but the clearance of hard-packed flood debris which supported the crumbling shale and served to stabilize the rocks' moisture content, has greatly accelerated the shale's desiccation and will cause further rock falls for decades to come. The observation of the preliminary 1977 survey, that the flooding of Ramesses III's tomb seems also to have destabilized several nearby tombs, must lead to anxiety concerning the future security of these monuments as well.

7. A HYDROLOGICAL SURVEY OF THE VALLEY, designed to minimize the effects of flood water has unfortunately halted. [9] None the less, the presently disastrous flood patterns around the tombs could be ameliorated with little effort. At the least, present-day archaeologists should observe the same elementary precautions as Howard Carter did, seventy years ago. As a matter of course, working expeditions should also install doors on their tombs that would not only prevent the entry of flood waters but also help to control humidity levels within the tomb. The survey suggested a design comprised of two parts, an outer set of doors built to withstand debris and boulders, an inner set to block water and humidity.

8. THE UNFORTUNATE HISTORY OF THE TOMB OF SETI I serves as a micro-catalogue of the threats that face the royal tombs. As fresh

as new when Belzoni first dug out its entrance, it was flooded within a few years and Mrs Belzoni accurately described the processes of destruction that accompany such a soaking and which, as we have seen, continue for very long periods of time. Throughout the following decades, as the tomb's rock slowly dried, further collapses occurred, providing a great convenience for the collectors of reliefs. The shifting rock also seems to have opened a fault in the burial chamber ceiling through which further quantities of water were introduced, staining the renowned astronomical painting and, in 1901, causing a partial collapse. Two years later, in an attempt to stem further rock falls, Howard Carter jacked up the limestone burial chamber walls and replaced the disintegrating shale of their lower sections with several cemented courses of fired brick. For some forty years the tomb remained relatively stable until, in 1959–60, the slow processes of desiccation were suddenly accelerated by the further excavation of hard-packed flood debris from the long tunnel that runs down from the burial chamber. Immediately, several of the tomb's lower chambers threatened collapse and had to be heavily buttressed; this, despite the fact that the tunnel excavations were more than a hundred metres away. In 1977, the preliminary survey geologists noted that Carter's brick buttresses were separating from the limestone and displayed a series of horizontal cracks. It is highly probable that this continued shrinkage is responsible for recent collapses in the lower sections of the tomb. Monitoring of these rock joints, however, could anticipate further damage to the tomb.

9. THE NEW, HIGHLY DAMAGING, ROCK MOVEMENTS which have been taking place in many royal tombs since the 1960s – and which prompted the 1977–9 surveys – are yet more alarming even than the unwitting piecemeal degradation of the tomb of Seti I. The preliminary survey of 1977 observed recent damage to tombs that had never been flooded with water; fresh faulting and rock movement that often displaces the plaster of the tomb decorations and which, in at least two celebrated monuments, has caused major damage. These new cracks puzzled the geologists of the preliminary survey. They suggested the possibility of seismic activity in the area. However, Curtis's full geological survey

established that there has been no movement at all in the major rock faults of the Valley during historical times: that seismic activity, therefore, is not to blame. Clearly then, the mechanisms of these new rock movements within the tombs are relatively small and localized phenomena triggered by a recent geological event or events.

10. THE TOMB OF RAMESSES I stands as a good example of this problem. In the 1960s the amiable monument, which had supported tourism and the occasional mild episode of flooding for a century and a half, suddenly sustained major new cracks. Sections of the wall paintings were loosened, and blocks of the ceiling fell onto the sarcophagus.

11. THE SINGLE EVENT OF SUFFICIENT MAGNITUDE that could account for these new and widespread rock movements during this same short span of time is the establishment of the Rest House cess pit at the Valley's centre. Since the early 1960s, this has facilitated an infiltration of thousands of litres of water through the fissured limestone and its underlying shale. One tomb, KV 5, has been directly flooded by the installation. Experience shows that the introduction of such volumes of subterranean water into the Valley will torment the tombs for a considerable time to come. Both the continuation of this infiltration or, alternatively, its sudden cessation, will fuel the dynamic processes of expansion and contraction that so affect the alignments of the Valley's rocks and the tombs that are cut in them. Many celebrated monuments have already been damaged: both they and many others are now under threat. These continuing rock movements should be monitored: photographic archives should document the present state of all the tomb walls; stress and humidity gauges should be placed in the tombs. Thus areas of potential damage may be isolated, splitting walls and spalling ceilings consolidated and detaching paintings carefully conserved.

Again, it must be emphasized that, as experience shows, these long processes of damage and destruction are so slow that, were we ignorant of them still, we could shrug off all future episodes as being merely the consequences of the hands of time or tourists, or that other bogeyman the 'water table'. [10] As the surveys of

1977–9 demonstrated, however, as far as the Valley of the Kings is concerned, none of these third parties presently figure large in the Valley's ongoing slow collapse; responsibility now rests firmly in the hands of its archaeologists.

12. CONCLUSION. Future flash floods in the Royal Valley will cause its tombs immense damage and destruction and their control must remain the supreme challenge for Valley conservationists. Archaeologists should take cognizance of the fact that their work changes present flood patterns and that the tombs that they open are thereby rendered vulnerable to flooding. Waterproof doors should be fitted at every occasion of working in the Valley.

Correlation of the written records of the last two centuries with the results of the 1977–9 surveys underlines the extreme sensitivity of the royal tombs to ongoing processes of expansion and contraction in the Valley's rock. The present situation of the Valley and its tombs resembles the fragments of a smashed tile on a drying sponge; the slow heaving and contraction of the fractured architecture of the tombs reflecting the slightest underlying changes in humidity. The closing of the cess pit and the opening and drying of any tombs such as KV 5, that are connected to it, requires precise monitoring throughout large sections of the Valley and its tombs. Monitoring that should continue for decades. Similarly, rapid desiccation prompted by the excavation of hard–packed flood debris from a tomb – the clearance, for example, of tombs such as those of Bay or Amenmesse or Ramesses II – not only threatens the collapse of the tomb under excavation but others in the vicinity, and this for decades after. Clearly, any activity that threatens to affect humidity levels in the tombs – the opening of previously closed tombs in the vicinity of others already in movement, is another example – should not be undertaken unless accompanied by long-term monitoring to indicate where inevitable future tasks of support and reinforcement should be performed.

13. RESEARCH AND RESPONSIBILITY. Of the seventy-five known tombs in the Valley of the Kings, more than half are only partially excavated and one third are completely lost from view. Attractive, famous and convenient, it is hardly surprising that the Valley has once again become a favoured site for small-scale egyptological

field work. But if future generations are to regard this renewed activity as anything more than the exploitation of ancient monuments in the name of science, the basic requirements of modern conservation must be met.

END NOTES

1. These surveys, funded by the Coca Cola Company of Atlanta, Georgia and conducted under the auspices of the Brooklyn Museum, were designed to provide basic data for a long-term conservation project in the Valley of the Kings. This paper's author was the survey field director. A preliminary report, 'Damage in the Royal Tombs in the Valley of the Kings at Thebes' was compiled in 1977 at the request of the President of the Egyptian Antiquities Organization, Dr Gamal Mokhtar. The reports of the main surveys of 1977–9, are contained in 'Theban Royal Tomb Project', San Francisco, 1979. Surveys mentioned below are: 'The Geology of the Valley of the Kings, Thebes, Egypt' by Garniss H. Curtis (Curtis) with accompanying map; 'Superficial Geology of the Valley of the Kings, Luxor, Egypt' by Marc Monaghan (Monaghan), also with a map; 'A History of Floods in the Valley of the Kings' by John Romer (Romer). This report was presented to officers of the EAO and others were deposited at the libraries of Chicago House, Luxor, the German Institute at Cairo and several other egyptological institutions in Europe and the USA.

2. Curtis p. 3. This detailed survey supersedes all earlier accounts of the area. Curtis p. 6, for example, notes that though previous surveys describe the Esna shale within the Theban Formation as being 120 metres in depth, in reality, in the Valley of the Kings, it is never more than 90 metres and usually less.

3. Curtis appendix; these being a continuation of earlier tests conducted by Earth Systems Consultants of Palo Alto, California.

4. The tomb makers made provision for these dangerous processes of initial desiccation, often by placing wooden lintels over door jambs.

5. Curtis has identified and named the major rock faults around the Royal Valley. Curtis p. 18 also notes that the tomb makers' predilection for employing rock faults as points of entry for tomb quarrying greatly heightens the tomb's vulnerability to water infiltration.

6. Romer p. 10 quotes Carter's unpublished description of the last known flood in the Royal Valley, on 25 October 1918. All subsequent data on flood patterns in the Valley is derived from Romer.

7. Monaghan's geologic map shows that a quarter of the Valley's lower slopes are covered with tailings – chippings quarried by the tomb makers and redistributed by archaeologists. These lie on mixed conglomerates brought down from higher slopes in earlier floods. Unstable when dry, they will form a potentially lethal rock slide when soaked by rain or flood; simply put, in times of storm, the Valley of the Kings is a dangerous place to be.

8. In 1979, I observed rain water entering this same tomb. Witnesses to the 1991 flooding, on New Year's Day, have told me that before it was mopped up, several inches of water lay in the burial chamber. UNESCO reports describe how flood waters were diverted from Sri Lankan limestone cave sites by a modification of the natural drainage patterns within the rock faults, a procedure that could prove equally effective in the Valley of the Kings.

9. There is urgent need for a computer-generated hydrological survey of the Valley. A suitable map – with 5 cm contours – was partially prepared by the 1977–9 survey; work that now requires extensive modification to show the numerous changes in Valley topography during the last decade.

10. Modern surveys clearly show that the Royal tombs are over 100 metres above the present water table of Gurna.

APPENDIX TWO

A HISTORY OF FLOODS IN THE VALLEY OF THE KINGS
(1979)

Paper written as part of the final report of the Theban Royal Tomb Project, 1977-9

Historians have constructed histories of the climate of Upper Egypt and Nubia and arrived at far-reaching conclusions based upon their hypotheses. [1] In fact, apart from a few accounts of rainfall, and occasional records of the height of the annual inundation of the Nile, the pharaonic record of climate of the region is very sparse, although it may be augmented by information obtained by indirect means. [2] In 1939 the geologist John Ball observed that, at that time, rainfall was higher in the Eastern than the Western deserts and commented that Assuit, north of Luxor, received a half centimetre of rain per annum while Aswan, to the south, had 'practically no rain at all'. [3] At this time there is no evidence to show that this pattern has changed, despite the presence of Lake Nasser. However, in the course of the past two hundred years, travellers to the Valley of the Kings have often recorded events of rain and flood in their narratives and, even from such diverse mixture of sources, it is evident that the Valley saw much more rain during the previous century than it has in the present one.

In previous geological ages rainfall in Upper Egypt was far heavier than in historical times. Some geologists would describe the present landscape of the Valley and the surrounding area as being of a transitional nature, that is, arrested in a process of transformation by erosion by water and associated debris, a process virtually halted by the continuing desiccation of the area. Although no rainfall records have ever been kept in the Valley there is plentiful evidence of floods and their attendant debris slides, and a melancholy history of damage and destruction in the tombs may be carefully documented.

144

Broadly speaking, the royal tombs in the Valley are divided by the location of their entrances into three distinct groups:

Group 1 consists of the monuments of the early to mid-eighteenth dynasty kings. These were usually situated under the retaining terraces that define the Valley and often close by clefts from which water would flow down in times of rain. Such extremely water-vulnerable tomb entrances were effectively sealed off by closing them with dry-stone walls covered with hard impervious plaster.

Group 2, mainly of late-eighteenth and nineteenth-dynasty tombs, are typically situated in the lower central areas of the Valley which are particularly susceptible to flooding and are directly in the path of any water that would drain through the Valley. The abandonment of the sealed entrance at this time in favour of hinged wooden doors further increased the likelihood of water penetrating these tombs.

Group 3, consisting principally of twentieth-dynasty royal tombs, were usually situated in the ends of rock spurs made by the erosion of two water run-offs during earlier geological ages. These tombs are obviously less vulnerable to serious water incursions and their siting was probably determined, in part, by the lessons of the unfortunate fate of so many of the Group 2 tombs.

From this brief description of the royal tombs above, it would seem likely that the locations of most of the royal, and decorated, tombs were placed with an eye to their security in times of flood. This was especially true during the later phases of tomb excavation when the desire for greater accessibility, as evidenced by the introduction of wooden doors, was carefully balanced by the thoughtfully placed entrances of the Group 3 tombs. However, virtually every example of the Group 3 tombs shows some evidence of penetration by water through the door. Water also entered the tombs from cracks in their ceilings, this being a particularly vulnerable route in many tombs whose locations were chosen by the ancient masons for their proximity to rock joints which made the work of quarrying and tomb cutting much more convenient.

In the ancient records there are a few references to rainfall in the Valley and the surrounding area. The most celebrated is a long twentieth-dynasty text scratched on the cliffs of the Western Valley of the Kings by the scribe Amennakht who records a visit to that remote place that he made in the company of his children to see a waterfall dropping from the terrace down on to the Valley floor. [4] Dramatic evidence of severe ancient rains which were accompanied by massive debris slides may be seen at the head of the Valley, below the tomb of Tuthmosis III, where the base of the cliffs is gouged and heavily stained by water. During the eighteenth dynasty, the Valley floor in this area had been close to bedrock, as the Carter excavations in the area made abundantly clear. [5] Entrance stairways for tombs were cut straight down from the limestone Valley floor and foundation deposits too were cut into the bedrock. But at some time towards the end of the eighteenth dynasty the topography underwent a most dramatic change. The Valley floor was deeply buried by a large amount of coarse flood debris which had swept down from the terrace above. This debris, finally completely cleared away by Carter's excavations in the early part of the century, sealed the eighteenth-dynasty archeological material under some five metres of debris and covered the entrances to many of the tombs. In photographs of this part of the Valley, taken before Carter's excavations, the huge slope of debris that came off the cliff above the Valley floor may be clearly seen. [6] Many of the great archaeological discoveries made in the Valley have been found under such flood debris or the water-cemented tailings of ancient excavations. Some graffiti [7] of the early nineteenth dynasty in the vicinity of this scene were scratched some six metres above the eighteenth-dynasty levels and indicate the approximate date of this catastrophe. This same flooding may have also been responsible for the partial destruction of some of the Group 2 tombs, thus influencing the choice of the sitings for the tombs of Group 3.

The tomb of Ramesses II, situated in a Group 2 location, was heavily flooded, probably early on in its history and, indeed, may well have been part-filled with flood debris prior to the death of that king. [8] The absence of burial equipment in the tomb, and even of a royal sarcophagus, strongly suggests that the successive floodings of the great tomb may have begun before the death of the king who, as his well-preserved mummy would suggest, was certainly never subjected to the indignities of even a partial soaking. Many other tombs, such as number KV 20 and that of Ramesses X, were probably flooded in antiquity and thereby rendered inaccessible.

Out of a total of twenty decorated tombs in the Valley, eleven were still standing open in Greek and Roman times and, consequently, their walls were engraved with the graffiti of some of these ancient tourists. The positions of many of these rough texts relative to the tomb floor is illuminating. Many of the accessible tombs were inscribed by the ancient tourists on all their sections down to the burial chambers, but when only the entrance doorways bear these Greek and Roman texts (as is the case with the tomb of Ramesses II) we may properly conclude that the rest of the tomb was blocked. In some of the other tombs the ancient tourists inscribed their names many metres above floor level; this suggests a previous deposit in the tomb of flood debris. These graffiti date from the reign of Ptolemy Auletes until the time of the visit to the Valley of the Byzantine Count Orion in AD 537, a period of some seven hundred years. [9] The tombs which suggest flooding by the positions of such graffiti are the following:

KV 7.	Ramesses II	4 graffiti, doorway only.
KV 8.	Meneptah	121 graffiti, first hall of tomb, one over a damaged area of decoration.
KV 15.	Seti II	59 graffiti, over most of the tomb, two to four metres above floor level.
KV 10.	Amenmesse	7 graffiti, in the upper sections.
KV 14.	Tausert/Setnakht	a Cypriot graffito, by the door.
KV 2.	Ramesses IV	56 graffiti, throughout the tomb. The position of the classical graffiti above those of the Christian period suggest a cleaning out of the tomb, the first 'excavations' in the Valley.
KV 9.	Ramesses VI	995 graffiti, throughout the tomb, two to four metres above the floor.
KV 1.	Ramesses VII	132 graffiti, situated as those of KV 9.
KV 6.	Ramesses IX	46 graffiti, situated as those of KV 9.

After this record of tomb accessibility in the classical era, the record of flooding in the Valley is blank until the arrival of European travellers during the eighteenth century. After a visit in 1799, one of the savants of the Napoleonic Expedition to Egypt, Citizen Engineer De Villiers, described light damage in the tomb of Amenhotep III, WV 22, due to rain water, which suggests that the tomb could only have been opened a short while before his party discovered the open entrance. De Villiers described the tomb as containing 'considerable portions of the plaster (on which the decoration was drawn) which were detached from the wall in such a manner that it was possible to carry them away, but we found that their fragility rendered their transport impossible'. [10] The results of this denudation by flood water are certainly visible in the tombs today. Many other tombs were flooded shortly after they were uncovered and opened. Indeed, the frequency of this occurrence suggests rainfall of a regularity which no longer exists.

Describing Belzoni's discovery of the tomb of Seti I in 1817, Giovanni d'Athenasi relates that he found 'a pit of about five feet in circumference and twelve feet deep at the bottom of which was a small aperture through which the water it contained had passed'. [11] It seems to have been this drain hole which suggested to Belzoni the possibility of an unknown tomb. In his own remarkable account of his work in the Valley, Belzoni also gave an accurate description of the drainage patterns and basic geology of the Valley, surpassed only in recent times. After forcing his way down into this drain hole Belzoni then gave his workmen orders to 'throw the soil into the well of the tomb'. [12] This well was a common feature in royal tombs, a huge pit in the main corridor which had, by containing the flood waters as they entered the tombs, saved many of the lower sections of the royal tombs from severe damage. By filling the well with this loose soil Belzoni, the discoverer of a pristine royal tomb, inadvertently became the agent of its first disaster. Within the year the tomb was flooded to its furthest extremities by 'a terrible rain which fell at this place'. Belzoni, whilst not recording his own blunder, wrote that 'water penetrated the tomb and ever since the stone has suffered greatly from the damp'. When the water penetrated down into the tomb it passed through, in Belzoni's own words, 'the beautiful solid calcerous stone' into a 'kind of black rotten slate which crumbles into dust only by touching'. The massive expansion of this underlying shale caused considerable damage (in the burial chamber), bringing down sections of the roof and splitting some of the finely decorated columns into conveniently sized portions that were eagerly carried off by the egyptological expeditions of those times. In 1825 an English artist, James Burton, 'made artificial channels and mounds around the tomb of Seti I to protect it from flooding as had happened some years earlier'. [13] The effects of the flooding was still being felt in 1906 when further sections of the burial chamber roof fell down, presumably following further desiccation of the shale. These deepest chambers are still in movement today and further severe damage must be predicted.

Noting further examples of heavy rainfall in the Valley, Belzoni recorded that the road built from the Valley to facilitate the removal of the sarcophagus of King Ramesses III was twice washed away by floods in the 1820s. He further observed that, 'rain falls very seldom, perhaps not more than once or twice a year', a far higher average than one might comment upon today. Sir John Gardiner Wilkinson, in his guide to Thebes of 1835, gives us further detailed information upon the conditions prevailing in the tombs at that time, and, with the exception of those uncovered by Belzoni, his observations of the fill in the tombs confirm the indications provided by the positions of the classical graffiti. [14] During the great age of archaeological discoveries in the Valley, that is from 1883 until 1913, there are no direct accounts of flooding and many of the tombs that were uncovered during that time were left open and extremely vulnerable to water damage, and have remained so ever since. A succession of travel books inadvertently inform us that little was damaged by water in the Valley between Wilkinson's time up to the turn of the century.

However, the guidebook of Arthur Weigall, published in 1910, records that the tomb of Ramesses III was closed 'beyond the pillared hall', where the 'scenes were damaged', also that the tomb of the Chancellor Bay (KV 13) had been recently partly filled with flood debris. [15] Depressingly, he also records that the tombs KV 38 and 42, excavated just a few years earlier, had been recently damaged by water. There had been considerable damage caused by water in the Valley between 1898, when tourists could still write in admiration of the lower sections of the tomb of Ramesses III, and the times of Weigall's visits to the site in 1905–10. The tomb of Ramesses III may well have been flooded from a crack in the roof [16] but this was certainly not the case with the tomb of Tuthmosis I, KV 38, which was filled directly from its mouth to a depth of more than 40 cm with fine sand, that was carried down from the terrace above it. Other tombs in the vicinity of KV 38 also show evidence of water intrusion. Some, such as the tomb of Tausert and Setnakht, have the distinctive yellow sand laying in large piles in their chambers and corridors but the route of entry in these examples has frequently been through joints in the tombs' ceilings.

During the excavation of the famous cache of grave goods found in tomb KV 55 in January 1907, as he felt beneath the rotten golden coffin of a queen, Gaston Maspero exclaimed that he had 'found something you have never before seen in a tomb in Egypt'. Surprised, he held up his hands, wet with water. It had entered the tomb through a rock joint and lain in the tomb long enough to destroy most of the perishable contents. [17]

Certainly at least one major flood occurred in the Valley in the early years of this century. Pick marks cut in the wet silt in both the tombs of Ramesses II and Ramesses III indicate a forlorn attempt to ameliorate the amazing destruction that had taken place. Unfortunately, these well-meaning efforts further damaged the tombs by causing a quick change in the moisture content of the rock and, consequently, a sudden contraction of the shale. [18] One of these workers left his heel print in the soft wet mud of the burial chamber of Ramesses III, mud now rock hard.

During the clearance of the tomb of Tutankhamun, Carter was very concerned by the possibility of flooding in the tomb. [19] An indefatigable observer of the local scene for many years, Carter recorded floods at Thebes in three successive Octobers, from 1915 until 1918. In a letter to Lord Carnarvon, dated 25 October 1918, he reported that:

towards the sunset, as the desert cooled, there was a great storm in the North-west. No rain fell in the Valley, but from all the washes that ran down from the Theban hills, including the Valley of the Kings, there was a torrent which cut furrows four feet deep and rolled stones as big as two feet across. The locals were unable to ford the floods when returning from their work in the fields as the area was a vast lake. Yet no rain fell. Then, later came a heavy downpour, which was the edge of the storm whose centre had been approximately ten miles back in the hills. [20]

Descriptions of desert storms such as this abound in the literature of Upper Egypt, and tales of similar events, often heralding the catastrophic flooding of villages and towns that lay in the path of the waters, are common in local verbal tradition [21]. One such story tells that in the period that followed the Second World War a flood passed through the outflow below the Valley of the Kings and uncovered many corpses that were buried in the village cemetery there. These waters were said to be waist high.

A few years ago a large village close to Kena, situated some forty miles from Luxor, was virtually obliterated by a heavy flash flood. Earlier this year (1979) a disastrous storm hit Upper Egypt. One of the great old Nile boats, the MS *Delta*, was sunk, and parts of the ancient city of Edfu collapsed. A town near the ancient site of El Kab, Mahamid, lost many houses and it was said that thirty people were killed as a great wall of water swept down from the desert. The Valley too saw rain, coming in great gusts from the north, over a period of an hour. The Valley was heavily damped, the rocks left slimy with rain and decorated with small pools of water. An ominous trickle of water was observed dribbling down the steps of the tomb of Tutankhamun, the most vulnerable tomb in the Valley. Slopes and cliffs above the Valley were saturated and took many hours to dry. [22]

It has often been observed that, in areas prone to suffer from erratically spaced natural disasters, such as earthquakes or floods, there is frequently little provision made to ameliorate the effects of potential future disasters, and this is said to be especially true if no catastrophes have occurred within the space of a generation. Local memory of flooding in the Valley is faint, a slim recollection of events of a long time ago. But the evidence of the literature and the experience of geologists informs us that the Valley of the Kings is prone to flooding, has flooded and will certainly be flooded again.

END NOTES

1. Bell, A. J. A. 75 & 76 and Trigger, *History and Settlement in Lower Nubia* (Yale, 1975), are two recent examples.

2. For a useful discussion of this see Butzer, *Early Hydraulic Civilization in Egypt* (Chicago, 1977).

3. Ball, *Contributions to the Geology of Egypt* (Cairo, 1939).

4. Cerny, *et al.*, *Graffiti de la montagne Thébaine I & II* (Cairo, 1965), graffito number 1736.

5. Carter, MSS., Griffith Institute.

6. Davis *et al.*, *The Tomb of Harmharbi and Toutankhamanou* (London, 1912), pl. 15.

7. Cerny, *op. cit.*, pl. 2461, 2501–4.

8. Described in Romer and Rutherford and Chekene, 'Damage in the Royal Tombs in the Valley of the Kings at Thebes' (unpublished, 1977), pp. 22 ff.

9. These collected and numbered by Baillet, MIFAO 42 (Cairo, 1926).

10. Quoted in Legrain, *Les Pas de Napoléon* (Paris, 1904).

11. d'Athenasi, *A Brief Account of the Researches and Discoveries in Upper Egypt, Made under the Direction of Henry Salt Esq* (London, 1836), pp. 12–15.

12. Belzoni, *Narrative of the Operations and Recent Discoveries within the Pyramids, Temples, Tombs and Excavations in Egypt and Nubia* (London, 1822), p. 231.

13. Wilkinson, *A Topography of Thebes* (London, 1835).

14. Wilkinson, *op. cit.*

15. Weigall, *A Guide to the Antiquities of Upper Egypt* (London, 1910).

16. Romer *et al.*, *op. cit.*, pp. 36–8.

17. Smith, *Temples Tombs and Ancient Art* (Oklahoma, 1956).

18. A mechanism of this destruction is described in detail in Romer *et al.*, *op.cit.*

19. Carter and Mace, *The Tomb of Tutankhamen I* (London, 1922).

20. Carnarvon, MSS., MMA Archives.

21. See, especially, Hume, *Geology of Egypt I* (Cairo, 1925).

22. Noted upon 3 May 1979, after 3 pm, when there was a severe electrical storm which lasted until after dark. Accompanying gusts of rain came up the Nile Valley from the north.

Bibliography

The Valley of the Kings has inspired a recent outpouring of specialist essays, only a part of which is worth recording. The brief bibliography below consists of works offering useful overviews of their subjects or alternatively, wide-ranging bibliographies. Further details of the scientific literature used throughout the book can be found in the notes of the two appendices. Other references listed below are those of works that we have cited.

General Works

Hornung, Erik, *The Valley of the Kings, Horizon of Eternity*, New York, 1990

Lexikon der Ägyptologie, eds. Wolfgang Helck and Eberhard Otto, with Westendorf and Meyer, 7 vols, Weisbaden, 1975–86

Porter, Rosalind and Bertha Moss (and Burney and Malek), *Topographical Bibliography of Ancient Egyptian Hieroglyphic Texts, Reliefs, and Paintings*, Vol 1, 2, 'Royal Tombs and Smaller Cemeteries', Oxford, 1964

Reeves, C. N., *Valley of the Kings*, London, 1990

Romer, John, *Valley of the Kings*, London, 1981

Works Cited

Preface & Introduction and Chapter I

Breasted, Charles, *Pioneer to the Past*, New York, 1943

Eaton-Krauss, Marianne, Review of C. N. Reeves, *Valley of the Kings*, Bibliotheca Orientalis XLIX 5/6, September–November 1992

'The pseudo-Asclepius' [24], (paraphrase of trans. by A. D. Nock, in *Coptic Egypt*, Brooklyn, 1944)

Lucas, Arthur, 'Note on the Temperature and Humidity of Several Tombs in the Valley', *Annales du Service des Antiquités de l'Egypte*, XXIV. Cairo, 1924

Lucas, Arthur, Appendix II, 'The Chemistry of the Tomb', in Carter, Howard, *The Tomb of Tutankhamen*, Vol 2. London, 1927

Chicago House: Rescuing the Past, (anon, pamphlet), Chicago, (no date)

CHAPTER II

Harms, Squyres *et al.*, Appendix I, 'Preliminary Geologic Reconnaissance, February 7 and 8, 1977' in Romer, John and Rutherford and Chekene, *Damage in the Royal Tombs in the Valley of the Kings at Thebes*, Brooklyn, 1977

CHAPTER III

Belzoni, G., *Narrative of the Operations and Recent Discoveries within the Pyramids, Temples, Tombs and Excavations in Egypt and Nubia*, 3rd edn. London, 1822.

Brock, Lyla Pinch, in 'Nile Currents', *K. M. T., A Modern Journal of Ancient Egypt*, Winter 91–92

Burton, Henry (Harry), MSS, Metropolitan Museum of Art, New York

Canoco/Marathon reports, *op. cit.*

Carter, Howard, MSS, Metropolitan Museum of Art, New York

Romer, John, with Curtis, Monaghan, Ciccarello, Esherick, *Theban Royal Tomb Project. A Report of the First Two Seasons* (privately printed), San Francisco, 1979

Romer, John, 'History and Experience in the Valley of the Kings', paper delivered at the 6th International Congress of Egyptology, Turin, 1991 (publication forthcoming)

Weeks, Kent R., 'The Theban Mapping Project and Work in KV 5', in Reeves C. N. (ed), *After Tutankhamun, Research and Excavation in the Royal Necropolis at Thebes*, London 1992

Weigall, Arthur E. P., *A Guide to the Antiquities of Upper Egypt*, London, 1910

CHAPTER IV

Budge, Sir E. A. Wallis, *By Nile and Tigris, A Narrative of Journeys undertaken in Egypt and Mesopotamia on Behalf of the British Museum between the Years 1886 and 1913*, London, 1920

Cecil, Lord Edward, *The Leisure of an Egyptian Official*, London, 1911

Champollion, Jean François, *Lettre et Journaux Ecrits pendant le Voyage Égypte, recueilles et annotés par H Hartleben*, Paris, 1986

Cooney, John D., *Amarna Reliefs from Hermopolis in American Collections*, Brooklyn, 1965

d'Athenasi, Yanni, *A Brief Account of the Researches and Discoveries in Upper Egypt, Made under the Direction of Henry Salt Esq.*, London, 1836

Hughs, W. in Foaden G. P. and F. Fletcher (eds), *Textbook of Egyptian Agriculture*, Vol I, Cairo, 1908

Juvenal and Flaccus (trans. John Dryden And Several other Eminent Hands), *The Satyrs of Decimus Junius Juvenalis and of Aulus Persius Flaccus*, 5th ed, London, 1726

Mariette, Auguste (trans. Alphonse Mariette), *Itinéraire de la haute Egypte*, London, 1872

Mekhitarian, Arpag, *'Le sauvetage des tombes thébaines'*, paper delivered at the 6th International Congress of Egyptology (publication forthcoming)

Momigliano, Arnaldo, *The Classical Foundations of Modern Historiography*, Berkeley, 1990 (for Francis Bacon quotation)

Romer, Mrs Isabella, *A Pilgrimage to the Temples and Tombs of Egypt, Nubia and Palestine*, London, 1846

Sicard, Claude, *Œuvres*, 3 vols., IFAO Bibl. d'Étude LXXXIII, LXXXIV, LXXV, Cairo, 1982

Stanley, Arthur Penryhn, *Sermons in the East*, London, 1863

Thompson Campbell, R., 'Ernest Alfred Wallis Budge; 1857–1934', *Journal of Egyptian Archaeology*, 21, London, 1935

Winlock, H. E., *Excavations at Deir el Bahari 1911–1931*, New York, 1942

CHAPTER V

Breasted, James Henry, *The Oriental Institute of the University of Chicago*, Chicago, December 1931

Gardiner, Alan H. and A. E. P. Weigall, *A Topographical Catalogue of the Private Tombs of Thebes*, London, 1913

Veronese, V., 'UNESCO Appeal' in Emery, Walter B., *Egypt in Nubia*, London, 1965

Index